VATCH'S
SOUTH
EAST
ASIAN
COOKBOOK

VATCHARIN BHUMICHITR

VATCH'S
SOUTH
EAST
ASIAN
COOKBOOK

WITH PHOTOGRAPHS BY CHRISTINE HANSCOMB
MICHAEL FREEMAN AND VATCHARIN BHUMICHITR

KYLE CATHIE LIMITED

*For all my friends throughout Southeast Asia
who helped with this book and for my travelling
companions who first shared these recipes*

First published in Great Britain in 1997 by Kyle Cathie Limited
20 Vauxhall Bridge Road, London SW1V 2SA

ISBN 1 85626 247 2

Food photographs copyright © Christine Hanscomb 1997
Travel photographs on pages 9, 10, 11, 12, 15, 16, 18, 19, 20, 22, 23, 24, 25, 27, 28, 29,30,
50, 52, 53, 54, 56, 57, 59, 60, 83, 84, 85, 86, 108, 109, 110, 113, 114, 134, 137, 138, 140,
142, 143, 160, 162, 163, 169 copyright © Michael Freeman 1997
Travel photographs on pages 7, 8, 14, 17, 26, 31, 55, 61, 80, 82, 87, 106, 111, 112, 115,
132, 135, 136, 139, 141, 164, 167 copyright © Vatcharin Bhumichitr 1997

Vatcharin Bhumichitr is hereby identified as the author of this work in accordance
with Section 77 of the Copyright, Designs and Patents Act 1988

A Cataloguing in Publication record for this title is available from the British Library

Styling by Antonia Gaunt
BOOK DESIGN BY THE BRIDGEWATER BOOK COMPANY
Printed in Singapore by Tien Wah Press

CONTENTS

TAMARIND — Pulp extracted from the brittle pod of the tamarind tree is used, most often dissolved in water as tamarind water or tamarind juice, to impart a pungent, sour, lemony flavour that gives a tremendous lift to any dish. It is a principal ingredient of Worcestershire sauce. Compressed blocks of the pulp can be bought in Indian stores. A poor substitute is double the amount of lemon juice, but use this only if it is impossible to find tamarind.

TARO — This is a rather bland tuber used as a vegetable or, mixed with flavourings, as a dessert.

WHITE RADISH (mooli, giant white radish, daikon) — This root vegetable can be served raw as a salad vegetable or cooked, whereupon it loses its cool sharpness and becomes somewhat like turnip in flavour.

OTHER UNUSUAL INGREDIENTS AGAR AGAR — This powder, made from seaweed, is sold in Asian stores and used as a gelling agent to make jellies, both sweet and savoury, without the need to refrigerate the liquid. It is suitable for vegetarians.

BANANA LEAVES — The leaves of the banana tree are used to wrap ingredients for grilling or steaming. The leaves help retain liquid and add a slight flavour to the dish. They are now available in Oriental stores in the West, though unfortunately you will have to buy rather a large packet, probably more than you will need.

BEANCURD (tofu) — Blocks of white fresh beancurd, made from curdled extract of yellow soya beans, are usually sold in plastic trays in a little of their own liquid. These should be used on the day of purchase, but can be kept for three days providing the liquid is poured away and replaced with a little fresh water each day. Cubes of fresh beancurd can be deep-fried until golden brown; these are fresher and creamier than the ready-fried beancurd on sale in Chinese stores. Beancurd sheets, sold dried in packets, look like wrinkled brown paper and need to be soaked for 5–6 minutes before use. When wet, any torn sections can be patched together with ease. Red beancurd, sold in jars, is pickled or fermented beancurd. Its strong flavour is used for sauces.

COCONUT — The fresh white meat of the newly ripe coconut is much used in curries and desserts in coastal areas, where the coconut palm is common. It is the coconut milk and cream, however, that are essential to many Southeast Asian recipes. These are made by soaking and pressing the grated coconut meat: a first pressing produces the thick cream, a second the thinner milk. Canned coconut cream is perfectly acceptable; if milk is required, open the can, let the contents settle then pour off the thinner, liquid at the top; otherwise stir well and use the full cream.

Young monks in the pagoda on Mandalay Hill, Burma

Elephants, northern Thailand

FISH BALLS — These small round dumplings made from fish and flour may be bought in Chinese stores and are used as a cooking ingredient, nearly always with noodles.

BLACK BEANS — These are just that, black beans, sold under that name in Chinese stores. In truth, these particular beans are mainly selected for their colour and could be replaced with almost any firm small bean, whether red, white or whatever. You can buy black beans in vacuum packs and they can be kept for a very long time in a well-sealed preserving jar, in a cool dark place.

MUSHROOMS — The mushroom most used in Asian cooking is the black fungus mushroom (cloud ear or *champignon noir*), usually bought dried and then soaked for 20–30 minutes at room temperature. Take care to remove any sandy grit and tough stalks. The smaller mushrooms are better. Dried Chinese mushrooms (shiitake) are the same size and shape, though slightly smaller than the common Western large flat mushroom. If no particular variety of mushroom is specified, any commonly available edible fungus will do: e.g. *champignon*, button mushroom, large flat mushroom (parasol), oyster mushroom (*pleurote*), straw mushroom.

PALM SUGAR — This is produced from the sap of the coconut palm and has a rich caramel flavour quite different from that of cane sugar. The best is soft and brown in colour, with a toffee-like aroma. It is sold in Asian stores, preferably in well-compressed cakes that are easy to keep. You could substitute a dark Demerara sugar but it will not have quite the same distinctive taste.

PRESERVED PLUM — This Chinese fruit, like a cross between a plum, an apricot and an olive, preserved in salted rice vinegar, has a very strong sweet taste with pleasing sour undertones. Scrapings of the flesh are used to make plum sauce. Jars of preserved plums are always available in Chinese stores.

friends, usually eaten as an appetizer with nibbles of chopped shallot, raw ginger, salted peanuts and coriander leaves.

While we did visit Chiang Mai occasionally, any farther north – as far as the town of Chiang Rai – was out of the question. And beyond, high in the Golden Triangle, the mountainous region that Thailand shares with Burma and Laos, was the world of the Hill Tribes, people ethnically and culturally different from us, living isolated lives in remote villages, much as they had for centuries, barely affected by modern life. When I was an art student in Bangkok the little I knew of these strange people I learned from a friend, Yod Chai, who came from Chiang Rai, and who was one of the few at that time to appreciate the highly coloured and decorated woven cloths and heavy silverware jewellery that the tribespeople wore. Yod Chai means 'Top Man' and, at a time when the rest of us were hung up on Western fashions – crazy about the Beatles and longing to visit London and New York – he was way ahead in loving natural materials, wood and dried leaves, plain earth colours and handmade objects. Whenever he went home to Chiang Rai, Yod Chai would bring us Hill Tribe woven bags, black and red waistcoats, and the round pom-pom hats that they wore, and would regale us with stories of their strange dances in a misty world of opium poppies and fierce warlords, stories that didn't sound quite real, more like ancient folk tales.

As for the Northeast, that was definitely a closed book. Indeed everyone in Bangkok did their best to avoid going there. Issan, as we call that huge region, was a notorious punishment post for civil servants and soldiers, a strange forbidding place of droughts and floods, of famine and neglect. Its people were not Thai as we were, but Lao, ethnically the same as the people living across the Mekong in the neighbouring Kingdom of Laos, as it then was. Of course, we knew what the Issan people were like, as thousands of them were obliged to migrate south in search of work, but their food was a rare pleasure only occasionally found on food stalls in Bangkok. Some years back an Issan woman set up a stall in our soi, or lane, offering what we always called Issan chicken, which was a half chicken, flattened out, marinated and barbecued, and often served with som tam, the highly charged, chilli-strong salad of grated raw papaya flavoured with chilli, fish sauce and ground peanuts, that was the one Issan dish you could find everywhere. What I didn't know at the time was that this fiery flavour was typical of a region where any food product was usually in short supply. With little meat and few vegetables, what there was needed to be highly spiced in order to help consume lots of rice – again sticky rice – in order to feed a family with limited resources. This meagre regime had to be augmented with whatever was available: frogs and insects – anything nutritious in fact.

The South, the narrow isthmus leading down to Malaysia, was different again. If anything, the land beyond our seaside holiday village of Hua Hin was even more remote than Issan. We were told that this was a place of bandits and danger – even the little old train from Bangkok to Singapore was thought to be unsafe. By

Winowing rice

Transplanting rice

reputation, the South was a languid sort of place, with palm-fringed islands, unspoiled because unvisited, and certainly with fascinating food. We knew about the Mussaman curry – an exotic delight in Bangkok, its rich dry spice flavours and the use of the man farang, the 'foreign potato', both imported from Malaysia (hence the name Mussaman which means Muslim). The extreme South was the land of mosques and veiled women, and much richer, darker tastes, the result of the spice trade with India and the Arabic connections that came with Islam.

There ought, however, to have been a fifth region, as far as food was concerned – Bangkok itself, for it was obvious that the one place in the country that had any claims to a cosmopolitan life would have a far broader range of culinary styles. Since the days of Ayuthaya, the old capital of Siam, that was destroyed during a Burmese invasion in the late 18th century, a form of cooking has grown up that is far more complex than the simple fare found in the countryside. Originally developed for the Royal Court and the palaces of the Thai nobility, this complex cuisine consisted of successions of small delicacies, decorated with intricately carved fruit and vegetables transformed into fragile flowers, with exquisite flavours and unusual ingredients. These creations were treated with the same respect as the highly stylized performances of Thai classical dance that are considered the summit of Thai culture. This sophisticated food was in turn influenced by outside ideas, especially from China, brought by visiting merchants or by the waves of Chinese immigrants who settled and became the country's principal commercial community. At the same time, Indian traders brought dry spices and even the Portuguese played a part, bringing the chilli, originally from South America, which more than any other single element transformed Thai cooking and, on a lesser scale, the practice of cooking sweet dishes with eggs.

After the departure of the Burmese and the establishment of a new dynasty at the new capital of Khrung Thep, or Bangkok as visitors called it, elements of this once exclusive cuisine began to spread into the homes of the rich and well-placed, and when I was young even moderately well-off families with servants to help them enjoyed a standard of cooking that seems quite astonishing in retrospect.

Our evening meal – taken early, at about 6.30 – was quite an affair. Everyone bathed and changed into light clothes, say a loose cotton shirt and Chinese-style wraparound silk 'pyjama' trousers, while our main cook Khun Aat sat cross-legged in the smoky outhouse, cooking over a charcoal stove, as the younger girls, who normally minded the children or coped with the ironing, ran about fetching and carrying for her. Mother might be preparing her special nam prik in the modern 'show' kitchen inside the house, while father sat at the table drinking whisky and sampling hotter dishes that were brought out as they were cooked and which served as appetizers. Gradually the range of courses would build up on the table – a selection intended to balance flavours, textures and heat – mother's spicy dip and a light soup to balance it, a curry such as Gaeng Kiow Wan Nua (Beef in Green Curry with Coconut, see page 40), always a special favourite, perhaps further counterbalanced by a sweeter dish. Ideally, there would also be a vegetable dish and some sort of fish or seafood.

When all was served, the cry of 'Kin kow' or 'Eat rice', the classic call to food, would summon me and my four brothers to table with father, while my mother and sister supervised the ladling out of a fairly large mountain of rice for each of us. From then on everything was shared, with each taking just a little of whatever dish we wanted with our own spoons, carrying it back to eat with the rice. We always ate with forks and spoons – chopsticks were Chinese and only for noodles – and we never heaped lots of different things on our plates at the same time – just a little bit of this, then that, taking it easy, letting it digest, as we talked and laughed about the shared news of the day. We always finished our rice, after which there would be fresh fruit – mangoes, rose apples, star fruit, whatever was in season. Occasionally, there was also a sweet pudding: either 'dry', like Kow Niew Tat (Sweet Sticky Rice Cakes, see page 47), or 'wet', like Kai Wan (Sweet Ginger Eggs, see page 48).

Eating out was a different matter – on important occasions we nearly always went to a Chinese restaurant, where a many-course feast would be consumed at a large round table with a revolving centre. There were some long-established Thai restaurants – like Vichit in the old government district near Democracy Monument, where civil servants liked to lunch – but for something special it was grand Chinese cooking that we preferred. Out of the home, Thai food was fast food – lunches and snacks, grabbed at one of the countless stalls that turned many side streets and market areas into open-air restaurants, or taken from passing food-hawkers whose pedal-wagons roamed the back streets of the capital, offering everything from fried rice to desserts and ices, in a continuously revolving circuit. If I went jogging early in the morning in nearby Lumpini Park, I could pick up some tou hou tod (deep-fried beancurd in a sweet sauce) for my breakfast, or sit at the morning food market over a bowl of Kow Tom Het (Rice Soup with Mushrooms, see page 41), flavoured with garlic and ginger. Other than that, Thai food was something eaten at home, and at that time it was totally unknown in the West.

All that changed with the war in Vietnam and the decision by the Americans to help our modest backwater kingdom protect itself from communism. As part of this scheme, Bangkok was made

Drying fish near Krabi, southern Thailand

the principal rest and recreation centre for the GIs fighting in that tragic conflict. The result was two-fold: a massive investment in the infrastructure of the country, with new facilities for aircraft and with highways ploughing north to the Mekong, while at the same time hotels were opened around the country as visitors began to flood in, bringing with them the inevitable mix of good and bad. On the one hand, the country was opened up to undreamed-of outside influences, transforming the economy and providing paid work for tens of thousands who had previously been tied to the land. At the same time whole areas of our main cities were changed into red-light districts, exaggerating the exodus from the poorer regions, where the effects of this capitalist revolution were last to arrive.

Nothing was untouched by this whirlwind, not even our food. The original GIs may have wanted hamburgers and hot-dogs, but some were adventurous enough to sit at street-side stalls where they learned to like Thai food. If there was one dish alone which converted the world to Thai cooking it would have to be Pad Thai (see page 47), the noodle dish whose mixture of flavours and textures is quite different from Chinese cooking, blending dried chilli, pounded nuts, raw spring onion, lime and fish sauce, along with whatever main ingredient the diner chooses – from pork to prawns. This is the fast food of Thailand and many visitors soon come to prefer it to a Big Mac.

Despite the disruptive side effects, the American presence stimulated the economic boom that has made Thailand one of the new tiger economies of Asia. It began with factories assembling

Bangkok's notorious traffic

Japanese products, using our cheap labour. A few years back there was a hugely popular hit song that satirized this process; the singer pointing out that, while everything he bought was supposed to be Japanese, whenever he looked at the back it said 'Made in Thailand'. That was, of course, just a stage on the road to development, and today goods really are made in the Kingdom, though with the result that anyone who has recently visited Bangkok can reveal – the 'Venice of the East', a magical place of meandering canals, with a tree-line broken only by the golden stupas of the many temples and the gilded spires of the Royal Palace, has gone. Khrung Thep, the 'City of Angels', as we have always called it, has now overtaken its distant namesake Los Angeles in sprawl and pollution.

Our family house, which once stood peacefully in its own grounds at the centre of the business district, is now hemmed in by soaring skyscrapers. As I write, a new one is currently going up on the plot next door and, recently, after a bag of builder's tools came crashing through our roof, the construction company agreed to evacuate my parents to a nearby apartment block until work is completed. It is a kind of madness. It is almost impossible to get about by foot any more, and some of my friends need three hours to get to work through the near rock-solid traffic jams. One lawyer I know is driven to his office in a campervan, while he reclines on a bed at the back watching videos!

Traditional pottery

Nothing has remained unchanged. As the Vietnamese War receded and the GIs left, tourists began to take their place, and over 20 years this has developed into a boom industry, with ever larger hotels offering a mix of Western and Thai food. In the main centres, Thai restaurants opened on an unprecedented scale, with servants deserting the houses of the rich to find work as chefs, preparing the same variety of dishes, beautifully decorated with carved fruit and vegetables, the sort of fine dining that only the very wealthy and well-born had known before. And this cuisine has now adapted to Western dining habits, with different courses, along with appetizers, and special food for buffets. Whatever was needed, Thai food could fit the bill; because, unlike other 'local' cuisines, that had only a limited number of traditional practices, Thai cooking was already a broad international cuisine which had absorbed many influences, from India, China and its nearer neighbours, and could absorb many more. Like the French and the Chinese, we Thai have a major 'international' cuisine, rather than a local one, which, in retrospect, makes its spread outwards into other continents seem less astonishing than it did at the time.

Of course, it was inevitable that, once they returned home, the huge surge of tourists from Western Europe and America would wish to sample again the food that they had enjoyed on holiday. The result has been the extraordinary explosion of Thai restaurants around the world. When I first came to London as a student in 1976 there were, at most, four Thai restaurants in the entire United Kingdom, trying to serve some semblance of Thai food without having access to all the necessary ingredients. When I recently helped found the Thai Restaurants Association in London we couldn't count the number of potential members. As for ingredients you can get most of what you need – from curry pastes to fresh lemon grass – at almost any local supermarket.

Much of the food offered in overseas Thai restaurants is basic Bangkok cooking mixed with the sort of Chinese dishes popular with Thai people. When I opened my first restaurant in London, The Chiang Mai, in 1981, I was determined to offer something a little more authentic, with a menu that included dishes from the North. Ten years later, when I helped launch the Chiang Rai in Manchester, we went even further and my latest effort, the Thai Bistro in Chiswick, West London, has a changing menu that offers a choice of food from every part of the country.

All this reflects what has been happening in Thailand since the economic boom opened up the country to its own citizens. Over the past 20 years I have tried to visit every part of my native land, enjoying its cultural treasures and sampling its local foods. With Thai Airways now covering the entire country, nowhere is off-limits any more. Many Bangkokians have beachside villas along the Western Gulf, while others fly to weekend cottages in the North. My banker Aunt and some of her friends have even developed a country estate in the mountains near Chiang Rai, and when I went to visit I seized the opportunity to look up my old friend Yod Chai, who had gone back to his home town after he finished his studies. I wasn't surprised to find that he'd opened a gallery-cum-shop, 'Silver Birch', at 891 Phaholyotin, the town's main thoroughfare, and that it is filled with the most amazing hand-crafted objects – tiny carved figures that move when you pull strings, hanging mobiles of fish and dragon-flies, tiny hand-beaten silver spoons with peanut shell handles. And the Top Man isn't alone: a thriving artists' colony has grown up in a place free from the stress and pollution of the capital, where people can still live close to nature. Yod Chai took me to the 'art village' created by his friend: Tuan Dachanee, now one of Thailand's leading artists, who has put together a compound of traditional northern buildings, all painted a deep black and decorated with animal skulls and bulls' horns, which gives the place an air of an American-Indian compound. Khun Dachanee himself always wears the same deep black and creates mysterious monochrome paintings of figures, half-human, half-animal, which he tends to give away to those he considers truly like them, while spurning offers from those he considers to be merely rich. His village, Nang Laer, is open to all, and if its creator is not away at one of his other studios in Europe, America or Japan, he will always take time to come and talk with anyone who wants to know more about his ideas.

Despite all the frantic development that has taken place, it is still just possible to search out such havens of tranquillity, away from the skyscrapers and the freeways, though this is becoming ever harder in the South, which more than any other region has borne the brunt of the unending tourist boom. Today, the remotest islands have beach resorts, and if you want to relax in peace you have to keep one step ahead of the developers. My last discovery was Krabi province on the eastern side of the southern isthmus, overlooking the Bay of Phangna, that strange stretch of water dotted with the awesome karst outcrops that rise sheer out of the waves, weird pillars of limestone that have survived where the surrounding rocks eroded away to leave only these towering peaks topped with a fuzz of vegetation.

Most of the people who make boat tours round Phangna come on a day trip from the holiday island of Phuket, which is probably the most famous tourist spot in Thailand. When I first visited Phuket, you rented a hut on the beach and fishermen came round to offer you their catch, which you could cook on an open fire. Today it would be hard to find a square metre of sand without a towel on it; which is why I wanted to look at Krabi, which is about to open an international airport but was then still 'under-developed' in the best sense. Someone suggested Ao Nang beach and, when I paid off the taxi, it seemed to be everything I could wish — a long stretch of empty sand overhung with twisted palms, water you could see through, and out in the bay one of the highest

karst outcrops in the region. The dream diminished when I saw the first hotel, a three-storey affair on the wrong side of the road away from the beach, but I decided to let fate take over and walked along the coast road, past beachside restaurants, enjoying the view and longing to get into my swimming things. Suddenly I stumbled on a vision from the past — well, almost — a resort, right on the beach, with individual wooden chalets — too smart really to be huts — set among the palms. Krabi Resort turned out to be the ideal compromise between modernity and those long-lost days of sleeping on a beach mat and cooking under the stars. That afternoon I shared a boat with an Australian couple who wanted to go snorkelling under the limestone outcrop. This really was heaven, with shoals of wildly coloured, tiny fish moving about us, some of them nibbling at our hands and feet — it was nothing serious, since they were much too small for that, but just a curious tickling sensation from dozens of miniature fish mouths trying to gobble up their dinner, us!

Khun Chuan, the owner of the resort, is a local businessman and politician who wants to keep the place the way it is, even after

Royal barge crossing the Chao Phraya river to the Temple of the Dawn

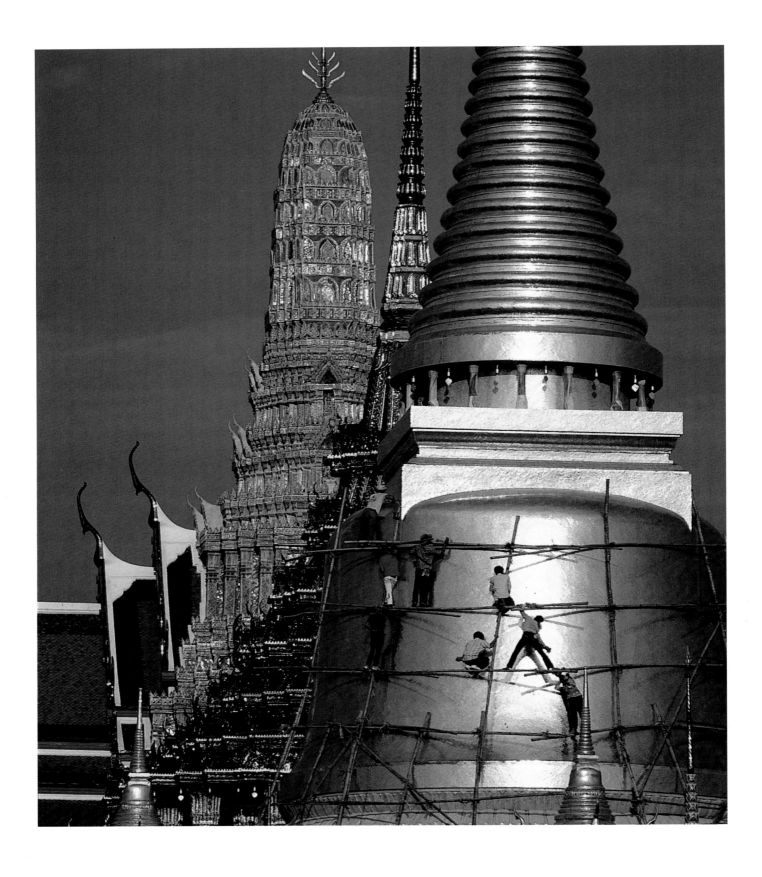

the airport opens and the crowds arrive. All the local people have agreed that no high-rise blocks will be built near the sea and that any buildings will be carefully integrated into the natural setting. I wish him well, though I'm glad I got there first, especially for the food, which was southern cooking at its best. The resort has its own Yam Krabi (see page 38), a salad with mixed seafood – squid, prawns, mussels, baby clams, in a hot sauce of chilli and lime, eased with fresh pineapple and crushed peanuts; and serves classic southern recipes like pork skin with aubergine and krachai, and the famous Yellow Curry Fish (see page 43) that is now eaten all over the country.

That, of course, is the main result of this opening-up of our country – not only do we now travel out to sample the good things once exclusively found in faraway places, but these same things are now part of basic Thai cooking. Our food is much broader and more varied than it was 20 years ago. Today you can buy Chiang Mai sausage in the food halls of any of Bangkok's leading department stores, and even the food of the once despised Northeast now has its devotees. Just off the busy Sukhumvit Road, the central residential area in Soi 36, is Bahn Lao which, as its name 'Lao House' implies, is set up as an authentic Issan stilt-house, with bamboo tables and chairs outside under woven awnings. There is the jovial atmosphere of a village party, with a folk orchestra playing traditional music and food so authentic even I have to be careful, making sure I eat plenty of sticky rice with the dishes like Tom Yam Gai (Chicken and Lemon Grass Soup, see page 32) which is heavy with the rich tastes of grilled garlic, shallots and a great deal of chilli – delicious but dangerous. The place is so pretty, with masses of plants in earthenware pots and patterned walkways made of earthenware tiles, that I strongly suspect the owner must be another of those northern artists.

There is a close connection between art and food in Thailand, especially when you come to the one section of our cuisine that is still virtually unknown outside the capital, and even there only to a select few – the highly refined Royal cuisine. I had one recent experience of this, thanks to my old friend Pan who took me to Genisha, a small discreet place at Sukhumvit Soi 11, near the Ambassador Hotel. Pan was a student of art history, specializing in Thai textiles, but has been many things since – model, antique dealer and, most recently, an organizer of grand receptions, including formal dinners at the Chitralada Palace for the King and Queen. Pan's knowledge of traditional costumes means that he can arrange banquets with all the serving people dressed as if for a celebration in the ancient city of Sukhothai, and he keeps in close touch with a whole range of highly skilled craftspeople who can quickly produce the breathtaking effects he needs. He has one group who can make a vast carpet of flowers in a day, so that the King and Queen and their guests can walk on a sea of sweet-smelling colour.

Craftsmen regilding the Phra Si Ratana Chedi, near the Grand Palace, Bangkok

Dried prawns in a southern market

However, the most important element at any royal meal has to be the fantastically decorated food, for which Pan works in close contact with the Ton Kruan, the title given to the supervisor of the Royal kitchens. The present Ton Kruan is the mother of Kuhn Montri, the owner of the Genisha, where he serves the same kind of delicate food created in the palace kitchens – the reason Pan took me there. Everything we were offered depended on what was in season like the hot and sour salad made out of crab-apple blossoms, laid on the plate as if you were meant to paint it rather than eat it and the tiny balls of meat carefully wrapped in fine noodles, with just a hint of a savoury stuffing. I've given an example of this sort of elaborate delicacy: Gratong Mee Krob (see page 36), a sweet crispy noodle mixture in tiny batter baskets, a recipe to test any cook's patience! And my recipe for Tod Man Gung (Deep-fried Prawn and Sweetcorn Cakes, see page 44) is just the sort of unusual mixing of flavours expected by the Genisha's customers, some of them members of the Royal Family.

To eat this sort of food is to leave reality behind for a moment, so it is a rude shock to step out of the restaurant back into the polluted hell of Bangkok's endless traffic, the worst effect of our mad roller-coaster ride from Third World status to economic giant. While many of the results have been appalling, our food seems to have gone from strength to strength, a sign that for all our rush for growth we have not yet lost our belief that life should be sanuk, that it should be fun. The task now is to put right those areas of life that have been badly damaged by the stampede for growth, and to pray that those neighbouring countries which are about to start down this same path will learn from our mistakes and be more careful of those precious things that are so easily lost.

GAM POO OP
CRAB CLAWS WITH SPICY DIP

INGREDIENTS

- 450g (1lb) crab claws
- 2 tablespoons oil
- 2 tablespoons light soy sauce
- ½ teaspoon salt
- 1 tablespoon finely chopped garlic
- ½ teaspoon ground black pepper
- 3 sprigs of coriander, leaf and stem, chopped

FOR THE SPICY DIP:

- 4–5 small fresh red or green chillies
- 2 garlic cloves
- ¼ teaspoon salt
- Juice of 1 lime (about 3 tablespoons)

PREPARATION

In a saucepan, mix first the 7 ingredients together, coating the crab claws thoroughly in the flavourings. Cover, place on a fairly high heat and leave for 3–4 minutes, shaking occasionally. While the crab is cooking, make the dip: in a mortar, slightly break up the chillies and garlic. Add the salt and lime juice and mix well. Remove the crab claws from the heat and serve with the prepared dip.

TOM YAM GAI
CHICKEN AND LEMON GRASS SOUP

INGREDIENTS

- 1 boneless chicken breast
- 450ml (¾ pint) water
- 5 small red shallots
- 2 garlic cloves
- 1 large dried red chilli
- 1 teaspoon salt
- 1 stalk of lemon grass, cut into 5cm (2in) lengths and slightly crushed
- 4 kaffir lime leaves
- 1 tablespoon fish sauce
- 1 teaspoon sugar
- 1 tablespoon lemon juice
- Coriander to garnish

This is a northern dish. The word yam on its own means spicy, but is usually reserved for spicy salads; when joined with tom, which means liquid, however, the two together equal spicy soup. Given the unusual combination of lemony flavours with the sharpness of chilli and shallot balanced by the simplicity of the chicken, this long yet manageable recipe is well worth the effort.

PREPARATION

In advance, prepare the stock by boiling the chicken breast in the water until it is cooked through, about 10 minutes. Remove the chicken and allow it to cool, then tear the meat into small shreds and set aside.

Next, cover the shallots, garlic and chilli with an envelope of kitchen foil and place under a preheated grill, turning once, until you smell rich charred aroma. Remove, place the contents of the foil parcel in a mortar with the salt and pound to a paste. Set aside. In a large pan, reheat the stock, stir in the paste and simmer. Add the shredded chicken and crushed lemon grass, and return to the boil. Add the lime leaves, fish sauce and sugar. Stir briefly, then remove from the heat – do not overcook. Off the heat, stir in the lemon juice (this must not be boiled with the other ingredients as heated lemon juice completely alters the flavour). As soon as the lemon juice has been added, pour the soup into a tureen, garnish with coriander and serve.

TAO HOU TOD
FRIED FRESH BEANCURD WITH SWEET NUT SAUCE

INGREDIENTS
- Fresh beancurd, see right
- Oil for deep-frying
- 5 tablespoons rice vinegar
- 4 tablespoons sugar
- 1 teaspoon salt
- 3 small fresh red chillies, finely chopped
- 2 tablespoons ground roast peanuts
- Coriander leaves to garnish

Different Oriental and health-food stores sell different shapes and sizes of fresh beancurd, so adapt whatever you can find to get something similar to this. Basically you need 4 blocks of beancurd measuring about 6cm (2½in) square and about 2.5cm (1in) deep. You may obtain such blocks easily as it is a fairly common size, if not, you will have to cut them from a larger block. Whatever the size; the beancurd will probably be sold in a plastic container, with a little soya milk to keep it moist. Remove the block from the container and place it on something like a baking tray to drain. Next take the 4 blocks and cut them diagonally from corner to corner to make 16 triangular shapes.

PREPARATION

Ensure that the beancurd triangles are as dry as possible. Heat the oil for deep-frying, gently ease in the triangles and fry until golden brown. Remove and place on kitchen paper to drain.

In a saucepan, heat the vinegar, sugar and salt until the mixture thickens. Remove from the heat, add the chillies and ground peanuts and stir until thoroughly mixed. Turn into a serving bowl, garnish with coriander leaves and serve with the deep-fried fresh beancurd.

JIN PING
GRILLED MARINATED PORK

INGREDIENTS
- 2 tablespoons finely chopped garlic
- 1 tablespoon finely chopped coriander root
- 1 teaspoon salt
- 1 teaspoon dark soy sauce
- 1 tablespoon light soy sauce
- 500g (6oz) (1¼lb) lean pork fillet, sliced into thin strips 5cm (2in) long
- Satay sticks

FOR THE CHILLI DIP:
- 2 tablespoons fish sauce
- ½ teaspoon dried red chillies, finely chopped
- 1 teaspoon sugar
- 1 tablespoon lime juice

Jin is a northern word for the southern Thai moo – pig or pork – and this dish is a sort of northern satay with a hot sauce. I have suggested the classic Thai chilli dip, but a whole range of hot sauces and dips throughout this book could be used instead.

PREPARATION

In a large bowl, mix the first 5 ingredients. Add the pork and turn them to coat them well in the mixture. Leave to marinate for 1 hour.

Preheat the grill to moderate. Skewer 2 strips of pork on each satay stick, line them up under the grill and cook until seared on each side.

Meanwhile, make the chilli dip by mixing all the ingredients well. Serve the pork with sticky rice, the chilli dip in a dipping bowl.

GRATONG MEE KROB
CRISPY NOODLE BASKETS

INGREDIENTS

**FOR THE GRATONG TONG
(GOLDEN FLOWERS) BATTER CASES:**

- 225g (8oz) flour
- ½ teaspoon salt
- 1 egg
- 225ml (8fl oz) water
- Oil for deep-frying

**FOR THE MEE KROB
(CRISPY NOODLES) FILLING:**

- Oil for deep-frying
- 115g (4oz) dried rice vermicelli noodles (see page 11), soaked for 20 minutes then drained
- 2 tablespoons oil
- 1 egg, lightly beaten with 1 tablespoon cold water
- 30g (1oz) beansprouts, very finely chopped
- 1 spring onion, thinly sliced into tiny rings
- 1 medium fresh red chilli, deseeded and slivered lengthways, then chopped into tiny pieces
- 1 whole head of pickled garlic (see page 15), thinly sliced across the bulb to make flower-shaped sections, then halved

FOR THE SAUCE:

- 2 tablespoons oil
- 115g (4oz) ready-fried beancurd, cut into thin slices, then cut again into very small strips, then finally diced into tiny cubes
- 2 garlic cloves, very finely chopped
- 2 small shallots, very finely chopped
- 1 tablespoon light soy sauce
- ½ teaspoon salt
- 4 tablespoons sugar
- 4 teaspoons vegetable stock (see page 14)
- 3 tablespoons lemon juice
- ½ teaspoon chilli powder

Gratong tong ('golden baskets', or 'golden flowers') are little batter cases with a savoury stuffing, usually served as appetizers or as party snacks. Mee krob are sweet crispy noodles served to counterbalance the strong savoury flavours of a curry or similar dish. Here, I have brought the two together, and the result could be served on its own as finger-food or, again, used as an accompaniment to curry. This is a long and complex recipe, but the results are very rewarding and impressive. There is a special implement for making the baskets, but you could use a small ladle with a 5cm (2in) diameter bowl.

PREPARATION

First make the batter cases: in a large bowl, mix the flour and salt. Break in the egg and mix well. Gradually add the water, stirring constantly until you have a thick batter. Leave for 1 hour.

Heat the oil for deep-frying, dip the mould or ladle bowl into the oil, remove and shake off as much oil as you can. Then dip the bowl or ladle into the batter to coat the outer surface and return it to the hot oil. After 20 seconds the case should shake free. Cook until golden brown. Remove, drain on kitchen paper and set aside. Repeat the procedure until all the batter has been used. Prepare the noodles for the filling: heat the oil for deep-frying and deep-fry the noodles until golden brown and crispy. Remove, drain on kitchen paper and set aside. Make the sauce: heat the oil in a wok or deep frying pan and fry the diced beancurd until crisp. Remove, drain and set aside. Add the garlic to the hot oil and fry until golden brown. Remove, drain and set aside.

Fry the shallots until brown, add the soy sauce, salt, sugar, stock and lemon juice and stir well until the mixture begins to caramelize. Add the chilli powder, the reserved beancurd and garlic, and stir until they absorb some of the liquid. Remove from the heat and set aside.

Finish preparing the filling: in another pan, heat the 2 tablespoons oil and drip in the egg mixture to make little dots of fried egg. Remove, drain and set aside. Return the sauce to the heat, crumble in the crispy noodles, breaking them into tiny whiskers and briefly mix. Turn into a large bowl. Add the beansprouts, spring onion, fried egg dots, chilli and pickled garlic. Mix well. With a teaspoon, place a portion of the mee krob filling into each batter case, arrange on a platter, then serve.

GAENG LUANG PLA
YELLOW CURRY WITH FISH

INGREDIENTS

- 1.2 litres (2 pints) water
- 175g (6oz) bamboo shoots
- 225g (8oz) fillets of fish (any kind of strong-fleshed fish, such as monkfish, that can stand up to being boiled without falling apart)
- 2 tablespoons tamarind water (see page 19)
- 2 tablespoons fish sauce
- 1 teaspoon sugar

FOR THE CURRY PASTE:

- 2 tablespoons roughly chopped lemon grass
- 1 tablespoon chopped kaffir lime rind
- 10 small shallots
- 12 garlic cloves
- 1 tablespoon roughly chopped fresh turmeric
- 1 teaspoon shrimp paste (see page 14)
- ½ teaspoon salt
- 10 small dried red chillies, soaked for 15 minutes then drained

Yellow curry is a southern speciality, thought to be particularly suited to fish and seafood as it goes well with the saltiness of such maritime ingredients.

PREPARATION

First make the curry paste: in a mortar, pound the lemon grass until well broken up, then add each of the remaining ingredients in turn, pounding well until worked into a paste. Set aside.

In a pan, heat half the water and, as it comes to the boil, stir in 2 tablespoons of the prepared curry paste (the rest can be kept in a sealed jar in the refrigerator for up to 3 weeks and used in other dishes). Add the bamboo shoots and stir well, then add the fish but do not stir. Add the remaining water and gently bring to the boil, simmer and add the tamarind water, fish sauce and sugar. Bring back to the boil, then serve.

PAD PRIK KING NUA PAD BUNG
FRIED BEEF WITH MORNING GLORY

INGREDIENTS

- 2 tablespoons oil
- 225g (8oz) beef steak, thinly sliced
- 175g (6oz) morning glory (water spinach, see page 17), cut into 5cm (2in) lengths
- 2 tablespoons fish sauce
- 1 teaspoon sugar
- 4 kaffir lime leaves, finely chopped

FOR THE RED CURRY PASTE:

- 2 tablespoons roughly chopped lemon grass
- 1½ tablespoons roughly chopped galangal
- 1 tablespoon roughly chopped kaffir lime rind
- 5 small dried red chillies, soaked for 15 minutes then drained and roughly chopped
- 2 large dry red chillies, soaked for 15 minutes then drained and roughly chopped
- 4 garlic cloves
- 6 small red shallots
- ¼ teaspoon salt

PREPARATION

First make the red curry paste: in a mortar, pound together each of the ingredients in turn to form a paste. Drain the chillies and chop them roughly.

In a wok, heat the oil and stir in the curry paste. When well mixed, add the meat and stir until just cooked through.

Add the morning glory and stir well. Add the fish sauce, sugar and kaffir lime leaves, stir well until the morning glory stems have slightly softened, then turn out on a dish and serve.

PLA NUNG MANAO
STEAMED FISH WITH LIME

INGREDIENTS

- 1 whole fish (trout, bream, carp, mullet or salmon will do), about 675g (1½lb), cleaned
- 1 whole lime, thinly sliced into very thin rounds

FOR THE SAUCE:

- 2 garlic cloves, finely chopped
- 2 stalks of coriander with roots, finely chopped
- 4–5 small fresh red or green chillies, finely chopped
- 2 tablespoons fish sauce
- 2 tablespoon lime juice
- 1 teaspoon finely chopped lime rind
- 1 teaspoon sugar

PREPARATION

Place the fish on a plate and cover with lime rounds. Bring some water to the boil in the bottom compartment of a steamer. When boiling, place the fish on its plate in the upper compartment and steam for 15–20 minutes, depending on the variety (e.g. trout needs less time than salmon), until just cooked through.

In the meantime, mix all the sauce ingredients in a bowl.

When the fish has steamed, remove and transfer to a serving dish. Pour over the sauce and serve.

TOD MAN GUNG
DEEP-FRIED PRAWN AND SWEETCORN CAKES

INGREDIENTS

- 20 black peppercorns
- 2 garlic cloves
- ¼ teaspoon salt
- 4 small dried red chillies
- Fresh sweetcorn kernels, scraped from 3 uncooked cobs
- 225g (8oz) chopped raw prawns
- 1 tablespoon fish sauce
- 1 teaspoon sugar
- Oil for deep-frying

FOR THE FRESH PICKLE:

- 4 tablespoons rice vinegar
- 2 teaspoons sugar
- ½ teaspoon salt
- 30g (1oz) cucumber, finely diced
- 1 small carrot, finely diced
- 1 small fresh red or green chilli, finely chopped

PREPARATION

In a mortar, pound together the peppercorns, garlic, salt and dried chillies to form a paste. Add the sweetcorn and pound well into the paste. Add the raw prawns, fish sauce and sugar and pound well.

You should now have a thick paste, which you mould into about 10 round patties about 5cm (2in) in diameter. Deep-fry the patties in batches in the oil until golden, then drain.

While the patties are frying, make the fresh pickle: in a bowl, thoroughly mix all the ingredients.

Serve the cooked patties with the fresh pickle in a small side dish.

KOW NIEW TAT
SWEET STICKY RICE CAKES

INGREDIENTS

- 85g (3oz) uncooked black beans (see page 19)
- 225g (8oz) uncooked sticky rice
- 450ml (1 pint) coconut milk
- 85g (3oz) sugar
- 2 teaspoons salt
- 225ml (8fl oz) coconut cream

PREPARATION

Soak the black beans in water for at least 6 hours. About 3 hours before you plan to begin, soak the sticky rice in water.

While the rice is soaking, drain the black beans. Place them in a pan with fresh water and bring to the boil. The water will turn black. Remove from the heat and pour away the water. Repeat this whole process twice. Bring to the boil for the last time. Check that the beans have softened; when they have, drain and set aside.

Place the coconut milk in a bowl with half the sugar and half the salt and mix well. Set aside. Drain the rice and turn into a small baking tray, spreading evenly. Pour over the coconut milk, sugar and salt mixture, place the tray in the upper compartment of a steamer and steam for 20 minutes. Meantime, mix the coconut cream with the remaining sugar and salt in a bowl. When the rice has nearly cooked, open the steamer and pour over this coconut cream mixture. Cover and steam for a further 5 minutes, then lift the cover and sprinkle the black beans over the surface. Cover and steam for a final 5 minutes. Remove the tray and allow to cool, cut the cake into blocks 2.5cm (1in) square and serve.

PAD THAI
THAI FRIED NOODLES

INGREDIENTS

- 4 tablespoons oil
- 2 garlic cloves, finely chopped
- 1 egg
- 175g (6oz) medium flat rice flour noodles, soaked for 20 minutes then drained
- 2 tablespoons lemon juice
- 1½ tablespoons fish sauce
- ½ teaspoon sugar
- 2 tablespoons dried shrimp, or 5 fresh prawns, or 115g (4oz) chicken, pork or beef, thinly sliced
- 2 tablespoons chopped roasted peanuts
- ½ teaspoon chilli powder
- 1 tablespoon preserved white radish (see page 19), finely chopped
- 30g (1oz) beansprouts
- 2 spring onions, cut into 2.5cm/2in pieces
- Coriander and lemon wedges to garnish

This is so much the classic Thai fast food dish that I have felt obliged to include a version of it here.

PREPARATION

Heat the oil in a wok or deep frying pan, and fry the garlic until golden brown. Break the egg into the pan and stir rapidly to scramble with the garlic. Add the noodles and stir well, scraping all the ingredients together.

One by one, add the following ingredients, stirring once between each addition: lemon juice, fish sauce, sugar, the main ingredient of choice, half the peanuts, half the chilli powder, the preserved radish, half the beansprouts, and the spring onions. Stir constantly. Test the noodles for tenderness and check that the main ingredient is just cooked through, then turn out on a warmed serving plate. Arrange the remaining peanuts, beansprouts and chilli powder on the side so that the diner can mix them in at will. Garnish with coriander and lemon wedges, and serve.

NAM PRIK GUNG POW
GRILLED PRAWN SPICY DIP

INGREDIENTS

- 115g (4oz) fresh prawns in the shell
- 10 small fresh red chillies
- 10 small red shallots
- 6 garlic cloves
- 1 teaspoon shrimp paste (see page 14)
- 1 tablespoon lime juice
- 2 tablespoons fish sauce
- 2 teaspoons sugar

Like all nam prik spicy dips, this should be served with a choice of raw vegetables, such as morning glory (water spinach) and pea aubergines, or fresh crisp salad vegetables, such as lettuce and cucumber. You can also serve it with small deep-fried fish, like sardines.

PREPARATION

Grill the prawns until just cooked through, then peel and devein them and roughly chop. Set aside.

In a mortar, pound together the chillies, shallots, garlic and shrimp paste to form a paste, then add the reserved prawn pieces and lightly pound (not to a paste).

Add the lime juice, fish sauce and sugar and stir well. Serve with a choice of accompaniments as suggested above.

KAI WAN
SWEET GINGER EGGS

INGREDIENTS

- 450ml (¾ pint) water
- 4 tablespoons sugar
- 1 tablespoon ginger, slivered into fine matchsticks
- 2 eggs

Eating an egg as a dessert, other than mixed into pastry or custard, will probably be an acquired taste for most in the West, though it was a practice introduced to Thailand by the Portuguese. However, this recipe is so simple and the ingredients so easy to obtain, it has to be worth the risk!

PREPARATION

In a saucepan, bring the water, sugar and ginger to the boil. Lower the heat and simmer until the liquid reduces to a light syrup. Return to the boil. Crack open the eggs and let the contents drip into the syrup with a circular movement of the hand, so that strands of cooked egg form in the hot liquid. The egg cooks almost immediately, so when both eggs are dripped into the syrup, quickly remove the pan from the heat.
Spoon the syrup and egg into dessert bowls and serve.

Laos

BUDDHA, LITTLE RICHARD AND BUFFALO MINCE

I expected many things from my first visit to Laos in 1994 — mainly the usual images of a forgotten Shangri-La, of cloud-topped mountains and faraway villages lost in the mist. What I hadn't expected was to end up in a brand-new discotheque on the night this isolated, landlocked nation took another lurch away from its communist past.

A monk adjusts his robe

The friend who picked me up at the airport had arranged lunch at a pretty terraced restaurant in one of Vientiane's surviving colonial villas. The meal was classic French bistro fare — pâté followed by a grill with chips and salad — and during it I got into conversation with the owner, a resilient Frenchman with a mysterious past that sounded like something out of a Somerset Maugham story. By his own account he had had a run-in with the criminal underworld in Bangkok before he made his way to safety in Laos. Now he was about to open the country's first real disco with non-stop recorded music. My friend explained that this was illegal as the government insists that live groups perform at least part of the time. Not only that, the new club would stay open long into the night, thus infringing an 11.30 curfew that was still in force. Intrigued, we decided to take the risk and accept his invitation to join him later that evening for the grand opening.

While I was a little surprised to be eating my first meal in Laos in a French bistro, I soon learned that this was almost inevitable — most restaurants exist for the expatriate community, business people and aid workers. Indeed, modern Vientiane is very much a French colonial creation, the remotest of France's Indo-Chinese capitals, a mere shadow of mighty Hanoi, the real seat of power. Vientiane is too new to be a major Laotian cultural centre and its main charm lies in the remaining vestiges of its former Frenchness — the occasional Anglo-Norman villa, people carrying baguettes home from small bakeries, and the French and Italian restaurants near the fountain at the centre of the town's tiny commercial district, where members of the small foreign community gather for their evening apéritif.

Until recently, the suppression of private enterprise by the communists meant that few Laotian eating places survived. In any case, hospitality has traditionally been very much home-based. When you pass someone's house in Laos, the occupants don't ask how you are, they say: 'Have you eaten?' It is the country's basic greeting and if you haven't, then you will certainly be invited to do so. Indeed you can always recognize one of the few Laotian restaurants by the presence of a water jar and drinking ladle near the entrance, a gift for any passing traveller who needs refreshment.

I saw some of these in the area round the main market, which I visited after that first lunch. The market buildings were dreary concrete sheds in the neo-Brutalist manner beloved of oppressive regimes, but the stalls inside offered all the usual colours and scents of Asia. At first glance this seemed little different from the great food emporia of Bangkok or Chiang Mai — piles of mangoes, mounds of small green aubergines. As I was to discover throughout my extended tour of Southeast Asia, the one thing that unites the region is the similarity of its markets. Every major town in every country has a huge central sales area, a large covered space, usually built by the government. The older ones are often beautiful wooden palaces made of soaring spars and arches, like the inside of an upturned boat. Newer models, like the market in Vientiane, are rather dull concrete shells.

However, nothing can repress the sheer exuberance of the sights and smells that confront the visitor once inside, for ranged along alleyways will be stall after stall piled high with the bounty of Asia. Particular products tend to be kept together, so you will get a cluster of vegetable sellers, with cleverly constructed arrangements of brightly coloured plants and leaves: pyramids of rich red shallots, sweeping curls of emerald longbeans, twisted fingers of ginger and galangal. Some specialize in one item, so you find stacked baskets of bright red chillies of all sizes, with surprisingly big and bulbous varieties — though it is the little tiny ones that turn out to be the most ferociously hot. Many things come in ready-to-buy bundles — five stems of lemon grass tied with a neat raffia bow, four little silver river fish carefully laid side-by-side in a round woven container. The fruit sellers have the easiest time: their heaps of lopped pineapples or purply-red mangosteens are irresistible. Every market has its meat section, with the butchers ceaselessly at work chopping and cutting — for in lands where refrigeration is still novel, livestock are always killed, sold, cooked and eaten the same day.

Indeed it is the freshness of everything, much helped by the endless splashing of water and the swish of hand fans to keep away the insects, that makes the market so tinglingly alive. There are cascades of cut flowers, orchids in huge bunches, and lots of

Fisherman on the Mekong

TAM SOM

HOT AND SOUR PAPAYA SALAD

INGREDIENTS

- 2 garlic cloves
- 4 or 5 small fresh red or green chillies
- 2 longbeans, chopped into 5cm (2in) lengths
- 175g (6oz) fine slivers of raw papaya
- 1 tomato, cut into wedges
- 1 tablespoon pickled or fermented fish (see page 14)
- 1 tablespoon fish sauce
- 1 tablespoon sugar
- 2 tablespoons lime juice
- Fresh firm green vegetables, such as longbeans, cabbage, etc.

PREPARATION

In a large mortar, pound the garlic, then add the chillies and pound well again. Add the longbeans, but only break these up slightly. Then, using a spoon to stir well, add the papaya and lightly pound, stirring occasionally. Add the tomato and lightly pound. Stir, then add the pickled or fermented fish, the fish sauce, sugar and lime juice, stirring well. Turn out on a serving dish, with the fresh raw vegetables. Any leaves, such as white cabbage, can be used as a scoop for the spicy mixture.

LAAP NGUA

SPICY BEEF SALAD

INGREDIENTS

- 175g (6oz) minced beef
- 2 teaspoons finely chopped galangal
- 2 tablespoons fish sauce
- 2 tablespoon lime juice
- 1 teaspoon sugar
- ½ teaspoon chilli powder
- 10 small shallots, thinly sliced
- 4 spring onions, finely chopped
- 2 teaspoon dry-fried rice (see page 10)
- 20 mint leaves
- A selection of raw crisp green vegetables, such as longbeans, morning glory and white cabbage

When I ate this dish in Laos, it was made with minced buffalo meat. Here I have substituted beef, less rich in flavour but certainly less chewy. You can vary the meat – chicken and pork would do, but my special favourite version uses minced Chinese roast duck.

In the original Laotian version, almost all the buffalo intestines and offal went into the mince, making it very nourishing. While I have stipulated plain beef mince here, you could be adventurous and add the liver, kidneys and heart if you wanted to get nearer to an authentic laap. In Laos the accompanying crisp green vegetables included young mango leaves, but these are unobtainable outside Asia, so use any fresh salad vegetables that are in season in your part of the world. This is another very piquant appetizer, which is good with drinks, though you can tone it down by serving it with sticky rice.

PREPARATION

Place the minced beef in a heavy-based saucepan and heat while stirring in the galangal, fish sauce, lime juice, sugar and chilli powder. Mix well until the meat is just cooked through. Remove from the heat and stir in the shallots, spring onions, dry-fried rice and mint leaves. Mix well. Turn out on a serving dish and serve with the selection of fresh crisp vegetables.

SAI UA MOO

PORK SAUSAGE

INGREDIENTS

- 10 garlic cloves
- 10 small shallots
- 10 black peppercorns
- 450g (1lb) minced pork (not lean pork: there should be about 20% fat)
- 1 teaspoon salt
- About 75cm (30in) of pigs' intestines
- Oil for deep-frying

TO SERVE:

- Lettuce or other fresh green leaves
- 4–6 small fresh red or green chillies
- Salted peanuts (optional)
- Fine matchsticks of fresh ginger (optional)

PREPARATION

In a mortar, pound the garlic, shallots and peppercorns to a paste. Turn this into a mixing bowl, add the minced pork and stir together. Add the salt, stirring well.

Pull the end of the intestine over the spout of a funnel and tie a knot at the far end of the tube. Force the mixture into the casing.

When there is 10cm (4in) of the mixture at the knotted end of the tube, tie a knot. Leave a small gap and tie a second knot. Continue stuffing and knotting until you have 5 or 6 sausages. If there are any air bubbles caught under the surface, prick them with a needle to release the air. Cut between the knots to separate the sausages.

The sausages should be deep-fried until a deep golden brown all over, then served with the fresh salad and the chillies to nibble on – you could also include salted peanuts and fine matchsticks of fresh ginger.

SOOP HOUA PHAK

COOKED VEGETABLE SALAD

INGREDIENTS

- 2 dried red chillies, soaked for 15 minutes then drained
- 6 small shallots
- 4 garlic cloves
- 4 hard-boiled eggs
- 2 tablespoons oil
- 2 tablespoons dried shrimp
- 1 tablespoon sesame seeds
- ½ teaspoon salt
- 115g (4oz) potatoes, finely diced
- 115g (4oz) cauliflower, cut into small florets
- 115g (4oz) longbeans, cut into 2.5cm (1in) lengths
- 115g (4oz) white radish, finely diced
- 175g (6oz) minced lean pork
- 2 tablespoons fish sauce
- 1 teaspoon sugar
- 2 tablespoons roasted peanuts
- A grinding of black pepper

PREPARATION

In a mortar, pound together the chillies, shallots and garlic to make a paste and set aside.

Shell the hard-boiled eggs. Separate the yolks, dice the whites and set both aside.

In a frying pan, heat the oil and fry the dried shrimp until crispy. Remove, drain and set aside.

In a dry frying pan, dry-fry the sesame seeds (see page 10) and set aside.

Fill a large pan with water and bring to the boil. Add the salt and the diced potatoes, bring back to the boil and cook for 5 minutes. Add all the other vegetables and boil briefly until they are just al dente. Drain and set aside.

Heat a dry wok and fry the minced pork, adding the fish sauce slowly to prevent sticking. Mix in the chilli paste and stir-fry until the pork is cooked through.

Add the egg yolks and sugar and stir well. Add the vegetables and diced egg whites, then stir well until everything is thoroughly coated. Turn out on a dish and serve sprinkled with the peanuts and pepper.

MOK PLA

FISH CURRY STEAMED IN BANANA LEAF

INGREDIENTS

- 6 small shallots
- 6 garlic cloves
- 2 dried red chillies, soaked for 15 minutes then drained
- 175g (6oz) fillets of cod or similar white fish
- 1 egg
- 3 tablespoons coconut cream
- 1 tablespoon fish sauce
- 20 holy basil leaves
- 1 whole banana leaf
- Toothpicks

PREPARATION

Preheat a hot grill. Place the shallots and garlic between two sheets of kitchen foil. Fold over the edges to seal and place this envelope under the hot grill. Cook, turning once, until the contents feel soft.

Unwrap the parcel and put the softened vegetables into a mortar together with the chillies. Pound to a paste.

Turn the paste into a mixing bowl, add the cod and break it up as you mix it with the paste. Break the egg into the bowl, add the coconut cream and fish sauce and stir well. Add the basil leaves, stir once and set aside.

You now need to make banana leaf 'envelopes' in which the mixture will be steamed (see the photograph on page 71). These containers will be pyramid-shaped and you will need two for this amount of filling. For each pyramid, cut out a rectangle of banana leaf, measuring roughly 30×15cm (12×6in). Round off the narrow ends to make a long oval shape. Place half the mixture at the centre of each, carefully easing up the long sides so that any liquid is held in and ensuring that these are slightly tucked in as you lift up. Bring together the rounded ends, squeezing them to a point which you fasten with a toothpick and which will give you your pyramid. Go easy with the banana leaf which is fairly fragile and can simply crumble if forced too hard.

Place both pyramids in the upper compartment of a steamer and cook for 15 minutes. Each diner should have a pyramid which is opened at the table to release the pungent aroma of the steamed curry, which is scooped out and eaten in small amounts along with rice and other dishes.

KALEE PED

DUCK CURRY

INGREDIENTS

- 175g (6oz) duck breast, thinly sliced
- Salt and pepper
- 4 dried red chillies, soaked for 15 minutes then drained
- 6 small shallots
- 225ml (8fl oz) coconut cream
- 2 tablespoons fish sauce
- 1 teaspoon sugar
- 1 teaspoon Madras curry powder
- 225g (8oz) potatoes, cut into small cubes

PREPARATION

Season the duck with salt and pepper and set aside.

In a mortar, pound together the chillies and shallots to form a paste.

In a saucepan, heat the coconut cream and stir in the paste. Continue stirring until a rich aroma is given off, then add the seasoned duck and stir well. Now add fish sauce, sugar and curry powder and stir well. Add the potato cubes and stir well.

Cover and simmer until the potato cubes are cooked al dente – no more than 10 minutes. Turn out into a bowl and serve.

KAI JEUN NA SOM

SWEET-AND-SOUR FRIED EGGS

INGREDIENTS

- 2 tablespoons oil
- 6 eggs
- 115g (4oz) minced pork
- Salt and pepper to taste
- 60g (2oz) onion, cut into small dice
- 60g (2oz) tomato, cut into small dice
- 60g (2oz) sweet pepper, cut into small dice
- 60g (2oz) star-fruit or pineapple, cut into small dice
- 1 tablespoon sugar
- 1 tablespoon fish sauce
- 2 spring onions, finely chopped

PREPARATION

Heat the oil in a frying pan and fry 4 of the eggs, sunny-side up. Place on a serving dish and set aside. Reserve the frying oil in a bowl.

Next, in a large bowl, beat the 2 remaining eggs, stir in the minced pork and flavour to taste with salt and pepper.

Heat a wok or frying pan without any oil. Pour in the mixture and fry, stirring constantly so that it does not form into a patty. When the meat is just cooked through, remove and set aside.

Add the reserved oil to the wok or pan and reheat it. Fry the onion until golden. Add the tomato, sweet pepper, star-fruit or pineapple, sugar and fish sauce, stirring constantly. When well mixed, stir in the cooked pork and mix well.

Remove from the heat and stir in the spring onions. Pour over the fried eggs and serve.

KAI PAD MAK PHET DENG
FRIED CHICKEN WITH RED CHILLI

INGREDIENTS

- 225g (8oz) chicken, thinly sliced
- Salt and pepper
- 2 tablespoons oil
- 2 garlic cloves, finely chopped
- 1 onion, finely chopped
- 6 large fresh red chillies, sliced lengthways into slivers
- 8 spring onions, cut into 3.5cm (1½in) lengths
- 2 tablespoons fish sauce
- 1 teaspoon sugar
- Coriander to garnish

PREPARATION

Season the chicken pieces with salt and pepper to taste and set aside.

In a wok or deep frying pan, heat the oil and fry the garlic until golden brown in colour.

Add the seasoned chicken and stir-fry until almost cooked through. Stirring constantly, add all the remaining ingredients except the coriander and stir-fry until the chicken is cooked through.

Turn out on a dish, garnish with the coriander and serve.

PAD SOM SIN MOO
LEMON PORK

INGREDIENTS

- 2 tablespoons oil
- 20 small shallots, thinly sliced
- 175g (6oz) pork, cut into small thin pieces
- 2 tablespoons fish sauce
- 225ml (8fl oz) coconut milk
- 2 tablespoons lemon juice
- 1 teaspoon lemon rind, finely slivered
- 5 spring onions, cut into 2.5cm (1in) lengths
- Coriander leaves to garnish

PREPARATION

In a wok or deep frying pan, heat the oil and fry the shallots until golden brown and crispy. Set aside.

In the same hot oil, stir-fry the pork, adding the fish sauce. When the meat is just cooked through, add the reserved crispy shallots, stir, then add the coconut milk. Stir well, then add the lemon juice, lemon rind and spring onions. Stir well.

Turn out on a warmed serving dish and garnish with coriander leaves.

HED PAD SOM PHAK
MUSHROOMS FRIED WITH PICKLED CABBAGE

INGREDIENTS

- 2 tablespoons oil
- 2 garlic cloves, finely chopped
- 115g (4oz) firm mushrooms (oyster mushrooms, for example), coarsely chopped
- 175g (6oz) pickled cabbage (see page 15)
- 1 teaspoon sugar
- Salt and pepper

PREPARATION

Heat the oil in a wok or deep frying pan and fry the garlic until golden brown. Then add all the remaining ingredients and stir-fry briefly, for about 30 seconds, before turning out on a serving dish.

Because of the saltiness of the pickled cabbage you will need only a tiny amount of salt and pepper, so taste the dish before adding any.

NAM VAN LOI MAK TENG
MELON IN COCONUT MILK

INGREDIENTS

- 450ml (¾ pint) coconut milk
- 4 tablespoons sugar
- 175g (6oz) melon (not too ripe), cut into 1cm (½in) cubes
- Crushed ice

This dish is simplicity itself, but wonderfully refreshing on a hot day. The Asian melon is not very sweet, which provides a slight counterbalance to the sugary sauce, so this could be a good way to use up a not-too-ripe melon.

PREPARATION

In a saucepan, heat the coconut milk. Stir in the sugar, bring gently to the boil, then remove from the heat and leave to cool.

When cool, pour into a bowl and add the melon. Half-fill 2 individual dessert bowls with crushed ice, spoon over the melon and coconut milk and serve. If you do not have crushed ice, chill the mixture in the refrigerator before serving.

KHAO TOM MAK KUAY
STEAMED STICKY RICE WITH BANANA

INGREDIENTS

- 225g (8oz) sticky rice, soaked for 3–4 hours
- 500ml (16fl oz) coconut milk
- ¼ teaspoon salt
- 4 tablespoons sugar
- 5 small bananas, each about 10cm (4in) long, cut in half lengthways
- Banana leaves or kitchen foil

You often see these banana envelopes on sale at bus stops and railway stations. No one really knows their place of origin, but the use of sticky rice suggests that they may have started off in Laos. While taro and black beans are not uncommon, the small sweet banana remains the most usual filling. When I was a child we used to judge the sellers by how generous they were with the filling – those who tried to get four slices out of a banana were never patronized again.

PREPARATION

Drain the sticky rice and place it in a pan with the coconut milk. Bring to a simmer, stirring constantly, until the rice has just absorbed the liquid, about 5–10 minutes – at this point it will be half-cooked. Add the salt and sugar and stir in well, then remove from the heat and leave to cool.
Make 10 rectangles about 25×20cm (10×8in) out of banana leaf or kitchen foil. Scoop 2 tablespoons of half-cooked rice on to each rectangle, flatten gently and place a half-length of banana at the centre of each patty. Make an envelope by folding over first the long then the short sides.
Place, folded side down, in the upper compartment of a steamer and cook for ½ hour. Serve hot or cold.

Cambodia

BRIDESMAIDS IN PINK

At the end of the 12th century, the last great ruler of the Khmer empire, Jayavarman VII, built a new capital at Angkor Thom, about 3km north of the ancient temple complex of Angkor Wat. At the very heart of this walled domain, the king placed the Bayon, dedicated to the worship of the Hindu pantheon, with each of its 49 massive towers bearing 4 vast heads of the god Avaloketesvara. Today, those eerily smiling faces stare down at the awed spectators below as the huge structure shimmers out of the early morning mist blanketing the dense forest which has now engulfed what was once, with a million inhabitants, the largest city in the world.

Sculpted freeze, Angkor Wat

Despite the ravages of time and man, the Bayon still contains some of the greatest art ever made. Its stone walls are decorated with 1,200 metres of bas-relief carvings, in which over 11,000 figures enact scenes from Hindu mythology or heroic moments from the wars in which Jayavarman drove the invading Chams from the Khmer lands. Truly awesome in scale and complexity, these stories unfold like reels of film that run at three levels along the outer corridors of the complex. On the upper level, Jayavarman himself – much the largest figure – is depicted as Indra, King of the Gods, enthroned in a floating pavilion, watching over his victorious troops who can be seen on the next level down, suitably transformed into holy Devas as they drive away the Cham demons.

Yet for all this swirling activity, the scenes that most engage the passing observer are those running at eye level which depict a simpler world of everyday life: servants bringing up supplies and organizing the camp kitchens, where they are preparing food in ways remarkably similar to those that can be seen in rural Cambodia today. A cook is about to pitch a suckling pig into a boiling cauldron, two men are grilling fishes held in strips of bamboo, just as people still do all over Southeast Asia. Nothing changes – even as the great army marches home from its triumph, wagons creaking, elephants trumpeting, two men drop out by the side of the road to enjoy a bowl of rice.

In the past it was the scenes of military prowess that were held up as symbols of Cambodia's glorious past; today one could

well take those more modest images of cooking and eating as an apt metaphor for life in the newly emerging nation, as it tries to recover from twenty years of abject misery. For the first-time visitor to the modern capital of Phnom Penh, one of the most striking things is the unexpected number of busy restaurants on its main thoroughfares and out along the banks of the Mekong, as it passes on its journey from Laos and Thailand to its estuary in Vietnam. Unexpected because all one seems to hear about the country are echoes of the horrors of 1975–9 and the agony of national destruction under the Khmer Rouge, and the subsequent Vietnamese invasion. Today, things are clearly far from stable and the tentative efforts to recreate a nation under an uneasy coalition of opposing groups may fall apart at any moment – and may well have done so before this book is published. At the time of writing, the country is again led by the aged King Sihanouk, who has controlled Cambodia's destiny since its declaration of independence from the French in 1953, save for a brief interlude when the Khmer Rouge took over the country. Today, Sihanouk is titular head of state, with the unenviable task of trying to hold together the opposing forces in the coalition, a task which appears to be undermining his health.

Politics aside, the country's main problems are the result of the unleashing of unbridled capitalism, fuelled by an influx of foreign investors which has given the once placid city something of the atmosphere of a frontier town. However, one only has to be taken, as I was, to the grim concrete school that Pol Pot used as his torture centre, to see that anything is preferable to that nightmare. After the school, I was driven out to the Killing Fields at Choeung Ek to see the mass graves and the high glass tower with its 8,000 skulls. As I stood in that terrible place I could hear the screams of the victims as if their souls hovered around the pitted ground. I hope they find peace some day.

Sadly the nightmare has not completely ended. Friends warned me not to travel too far from the main centres without armed protection against bandits and not to wander away from marked paths because of the countless land mines that are still scattered over much of the countryside. Having been told all these gloomy things, I was then driven across the new 'Japanese' bridge, along the Porimphorn Road on the banks of the Mekong, to the Hang Neak, one of a long line of large restaurants built on stilts above the river, its main room bedecked with winking fairy lights and loud with pop music.

When we got there we found a wedding party in progress, the bride in white lace, the groom somewhat stiff in his unfamiliar Western suit, the bridesmaids giggly in pink. As in the other countries of Southeast Asia, village people still have a traditional wedding in traditional dress, whereas city dwellers have two celebrations – a traditional wedding in the morning, followed by an early-evening party for which everyone changes into Western costume. Most people now wear simple Western clothes – trousers and shirts, loose dresses and blouses – for city life, though the combination of loose cotton top and wrap-around sarong for women, with baggy trousers for men, is still the preferred dress in farming communities.

Of course, young people want the latest American fashions and you see jeans and trainers everywhere. At another table in that restaurant there was a group of such teenagers enjoying Coca-Colas as a waitress lit the candles on a birthday cake covered in lurid red and green icing. And though it may appear tasteless to mention such things so close to the memory of torture and death, there is ample justification – frivolity is the best antidote to tyranny, innocent fun is the one thing no dictator can bear. The bustling restaurants of Phnom Penh are part of a healing process, a triumphant sign that the people of that ravaged land have a brighter future ahead of them, no matter what immediate problems they may encounter.

Twenty years of chaos have at least spared the city the destructive 'progress' of other Asian capitals. Phnom Penh still stretches languidly along the western bank of the Tonlé Sap river, just above the point where it meets the Mekong. The layout of the city is simple – two broad north-south avenues, crossed by five wide east-west boulevards. This simplicity has been somewhat spoiled by the recent renaming of many streets; the lords of communism, Marx and Lenin, have been pushed aside by the nation's monarchs – Monivong, Norodom and the present King Sihanouk. This tends to reinforce the first impression that Phnom Penh is a royal city and that its heart is the king's palace, above whose walls can be seen the spires of the silver pagoda and the throne hall and the burial stupas of the royal family.

The royal presence aside, Phnom Penh was really a French colonial creation, with wide tree-lined streets and handsome villas. Predominately ochre in colour, some are in Mediterranean stucco, others in the half-timbered Anglo-Norman style, so that from one street to the next the casual stroller moves effortlessly between Nice and Le Touquet. It is pleasing to note that Pol Pot's crazed attempt to obliterate all memory of the past by evacuating the city accidentally preserved a considerable amount of this colonial heritage, leaving far more of these lovely houses intact than can now be found in Vientiane. Happily, many of the newly arrived foreign businesses from Taiwan, Hong Kong, Bangkok and Tokyo are finding it congenial to establish their corporate headquarters in these attractive structures, offering some hope that the city may retain something of its former elegance.

In the twenties and thirties, when Art Deco, with its mix of European Modernism and folk elements from other cultures, became a universal style, the French graced Phnom Penh with an

Fishermen on Lake Tonlé Sap

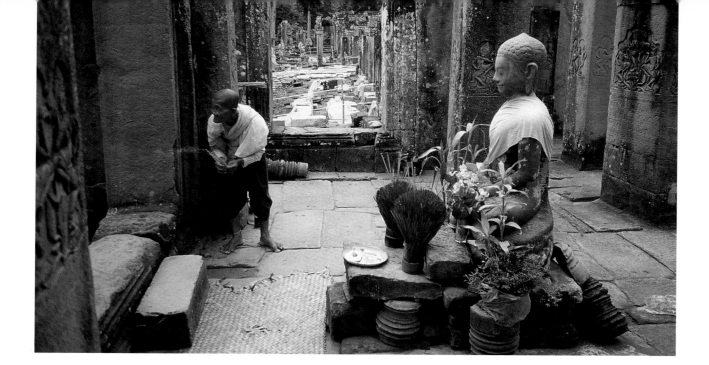

**Faithful guardian of a ruined
shrine, Angkor Wat**

distinctly glum until one gentleman among us quickly downed his first drink and called her back to order another, thus making everyone happy.

I spent three days in Angkor doing what the French dubbed 'the Grand Circuit'. This is essential if one wants to get some notion of the scale and diversity of the Khmer golden age which spanned four centuries, alternating between Hinduism and Buddhism, with each successive ruler trying to outdo his predecessor with the size and splendour of his buildings. To the uninitiated, it comes as a surprise to realize that the ruins comprise more than the famous towered temples and include royal bathing pools and a gigantic parade ground. It was there that the king and his court stood on a long terrace, supported by carved elephants and the mythical bird, the garuda, to watch their armies marching past, just like the scenes recorded on the walls of the Bayon.

Although one begins with Angkor Wat itself, there is no sense of passing from best to least as the days unfold; each part of the tour offers its own unique delights. I was there in May at the beginning of the rainy season, which most tourists try to avoid. I in fact like the occasional monsoon-like downpour, which seldom lasts more than an hour each day and often creates spectacular effects of light and colour. When I first saw Angkor Wat, it had a stunning rainbow arched over its towers, and the Ta Prohm temple which I visited on the final day was greatly enlivened by a torrential downpour. Ta Prohm is the one temple that the French restorers, who had long debated the merits and demerits of rebuilding the fallen masonry, decided to leave pretty much as they found it. This allows the visitor to experience something of the thrill enjoyed by the first explorers when they cut their way through the undergrowth to find these amazing buildings caught in the destructive embrace of tendrils and creepers, the walls inextricably locked into the trunks and branches of giant banyan trees, strangling the carv-

**Monks receiving offerings of food
and other gifts during a festival**

ings and holding up the roofs and corridors. There is a feeling of dread as one clambers over the fallen stones and cowers under arches that are enmeshed in the branches of a tree that is itself dying, so that it is no longer possible to say what is holding up what. I had no sooner reached the heart of this sinister fortress than the light suddenly plunged to purple and violet and the rain began to ricochet off the tumbled lichened blocks like hissing gunfire. Sheltering in a darkened cloister, I knew I was sharing the place with bats and all manner of insects and perhaps even the deadly hannuman snake. The scene was grand opera and Hollywood all rolled into one and only needed the sudden appearance of Indiana Jones to complete the sense of unreality.

Back in Phnom Penh and with a Sunday to fill before flying back to Bangkok, I was advised to make the short journey out of town, to what the Cambodians call Koki Beach, for a rare culinary treat. I was not alone! Almost anyone in the city with access to transport, from government officials in their Mercedes to clerks on motor scooters, seemed to be making for this spot on the Mekong where whole families rent little stilt shelters in which to pass the day eating, drinking, talking and sleeping. They can buy their picnics from stalls selling everything from grilled chicken to deep-fried crickets. There is every kind of pickle; the fruit varieties such as mango are eaten as snacks, while others, like pickled garlic, are used as cooking ingredients. To finish, there was a delicious sweet made of sticky rice and coconut with fresh jackfruit grilled inside a banana leaf envelope (see page 104). Everyone was obviously enjoying their one precious day of leisure. For the older people it was clearly a memory of the way of life they had known before disaster struck and a hopeful sign that the healing process will continue and that their children, who splash about so innocently in the river, will never know anything else.

MUAN DOT

POT-ROASTED CHICKEN WITH LEMON GRASS

INGREDIENTS
- 1 small whole chicken
- 3–4 tablespoons oyster sauce
- 10 stalks of lemon grass
- Oil

TO SERVE:
- Tik Marij (see page 91)
- Tik Prahok (see page 94)

Having ordered what was listed as 'roast chicken' in a restaurant in Siam Reap, I was shown round an ovenless kitchen and wondered how they were going to 'roast' it and how they were going to do it quickly enough for our dinner. Even when I realized that they were about to pot-roast it in a covered wok I was still concerned about the time factor, though in the end my fears were groundless as the whole thing was achieved in a mere half-hour, yet the chicken was cooked through and delicious; a plump Western chicken will take slightly longer.

PREPARATION
Cover the chicken in the oyster sauce, inside and out, and leave to marinate for 30 minutes. Place the lemon grass in a heavy-based saucepan just big enough for the bird, and which has a tight-fitting lid, and add just enough oil to cover. Heat and, as the lemon grass begins to fry, place the whole chicken on top and cover with the lid. Pot-roast, turning every 15 minutes, until the chicken is cooked through, about 30 minutes to 1 hour depending on the size of the bird. It should be a rich golden-brown when cooking is complete, and the juices should run clear when the thickest part of the flesh is pierced. Discard the lemon grass, quarter the chicken and serve with both Cambodian sauces: Tik Marij and Tik Prahok.

CHAR BAI MREAH PRIU

EGG AND BASIL FRIED RICE

INGREDIENTS
- 2 tablespoons oil
- 2 small garlic cloves, finely chopped
- 2 long fresh red mild chillies, thinly sliced diagonally into ovals
- 115g (4oz) protein of choice (pork, chicken, seafood, etc), cut into small thin pieces
- 2 small eggs
- 225g (8oz) steamed rice
- 1 tablespoon fish sauce
- 1 tablespoon light soy sauce
- ½ teaspoon sugar
- 1 small onion, halved and thinly sliced
- 20 fresh holy basil leaves

This is the Cambodian variant of a basic one-dish meal found all over Southeast Asia. The nature of the main protein ingredient is left for the diner to choose. Elsewhere, egg fried rice and basil fried rice are two separate dishes; here they are brought together.

PREPARATION
Heat the oil in a wok or deep frying pan and fry the garlic until golden. Add the chillies, stir once, then add the protein of choice and stir-fry briefly until just cooked through. Break in the eggs and stir well. Add the rice and mix very well. Add all the remaining ingredients in turn, stirring once between each addition. Serve immediately.

SAMLOR JRUOH
HOT-AND-SOUR MUSHROOM AND TOMATO SOUP

INGREDIENTS

- 450ml (¾ pint) vegetable stock (see page 14)
- 5cm (2in) piece of lemon grass, coarsely chopped
- 3 kaffir lime leaves, coarsely chopped
- 5mm (¼in) piece of galangal, thinly sliced
- 1 large tomato, cut into wedges
- 115g (4oz) small whole straw mushrooms
- 3 tablespoons lime juice
- 2 tablespoons light soy sauce
- A pinch of salt
- 4–5 small fresh red or green chillies, broken open with a single blow from a spoon or pestle
- Coriander leaves to garnish

PREPARATION

In a large saucepan, heat the stock to a boil. Add all the ingredients except the coriander, bring back to the boil and simmer for 1 minute.

Transfer to a serving bowl, garnish with roughly torn coriander leaves and serve.

SAMLOR CHANANG DY
CLAY-POT BEEF, VEGETABLE AND NOODLE SOUP

INGREDIENTS

- 1 litre (1¾ pints) rich beef stock (see page 14)
- 2 ducks' or hens' eggs
- 225g (8oz) steak, thinly sliced
- 60g (2oz) each local seasonal quick-cooking vegetables of choice
- 60g (2oz) Chinese cabbage leaves, roughly sliced
- 60g (2oz) morning glory (water spinach)
- 2 spring onions, chopped into 2.5cm (1in) lengths
- 10–15 holy basil leaves
- 2 stems of coriander leaves
- 115g (4oz) egg noodles, soaked if dried
- 60g (2oz) beancurd sheet, soaked

This is party food. In Cambodia, a clay pot on a portable charcoal burner is brought to the table and inside is a succulent beef stock. Everyone will have their own tik marij (page 91) or tik prahok (page 94) to adjust the flavour to their own taste. A fondue set or a 'steam-boat heater' would make ideal substitutes for the clay pot, otherwise you'll just have to eat round a saucepan on the kitchen stove!

PREPARATION

First make rich beef stock as per the instructions on page 14. Let the stock cool and skim off any excess fat. Then either remove the bones and serve the stock with the other ingredients, or remove everything, pass the stock through a filter and serve as a clear liquid. Either way, reheat and place in a dish on a heater on the table.

Each diner is given a bowl and chopsticks and a second bowl with an egg (duck's or hen's). The egg is broken into the bowl, slightly beaten, and the pieces of steak dunked in it before being placed in the stock with whatever vegetables the diner chooses along with some herbs, noodles and beancurd. Cooking time is a matter of choice, though it will not be long before everyone is eating whatever they can pick out of the stock, enjoying everybody's additions with no complaint.

YOAM MAKAH TREY ANG

DEEP-FRIED SMOKED FISH WITH RAW MANGO SALAD

INGREDIENTS

- Enough lettuce leaves to cover a serving dish
- Oil for deep-frying
- 115g (4oz) smoked fish (Western smoked herring will do), cut across into thin slices
- 60g (2oz) raw green mango, finely chopped into matchsticks
- 30g (1oz) carrot, finely chopped into matchsticks
- 30g (1oz) onion, finely chopped
- 4–5 small fresh red or green chillies, finely chopped
- 2 tablespoons fish sauce
- 1–2 tablespoons lime juice (this is optional and depends on the flavour of the raw mango – if it is very sour, you won't need the lime juice)
- 1 teaspoon sugar
- 1 tablespoon coarsely chopped coriander leaf and stem
- Mint leaves to garnish

Yoam is the Cambodian equivalent of the Thai yam, the spicy salad often served as an appetizer with drinks. The smoked fish is especially good in northern Cambodia, near Angkor Wat.

PREPARATION

Arrange the lettuce leaves on a serving dish and set aside.

Heat the oil for deep-frying and deep-fry the fish until crispy. Remove from the oil and place in a mixing bowl. Add all the other ingredients except the mint. Stir well and turn out on the lettuce leaves.

Garnish with mint leaves and serve.

TIK PRAHOK

PICKLED FISH DIP

INGREDIENTS

- 1–2 tablespoons boiled fermented fish liquid (see right)
- 2 tablespoons lime juice
- 1 teaspoon sugar
- 2–4 small fresh red or green chillies, finely chopped
- 2.5cm (1in) piece of lemon grass (the young inner stem, after the hard outer layer has been peeled away), finely chopped
- 1 teaspoon very finely chopped coriander leaf and stem

This is the second of the basic Cambodian dipping sauces, though much less commonly served than tik marij, which always appears at meals.

As its basis, you will need to take from a jar of fermented or pickled fish (see page 14) a solid piece of fish with some liquid and place these in a saucepan. Remove any bones from the fish, then break up the flesh and mash with the liquid. Bring gently to the boil, and simmer for a few moments to kill off any impurities. Allow to cool, then taste – if it is very salty, you will need to use only 1 tablespoon for this recipe; if not, then up to 2 tablespoons will be needed.

PREPARATION

Place all the ingredients in a mixing bowl and stir well. Transfer to a single serving dish or to smaller individual dipping dishes.

TROP BAMPORNG JIAMUAY PONG TIA
FRIED AUBERGINE WITH EGG

INGREDIENTS

- 2 large ducks' eggs or 4 medium hens' eggs
- 1 large whole purple aubergine, sliced across into thin rounds
- 3 tablespoons oil
- 1 tablespoon fish sauce (soy sauce if vegetarian)
- A grinding of black pepper
- ½ teaspoon sugar
- 2 medium spring onions, finely chopped

PREPARATION

Break 1 of the ducks' eggs or 2 hens' eggs into a mixing bowl and beat. Add the aubergine slices and coat well in the egg.

Heat 2 tablespoons of the oil in a wok or deep frying pan and fry the coated aubergine slices until golden and crispy. Remove from the oil and set aside.

Add the remaining tablespoon of oil to the pan, heat and break in the remaining egg(s). As they begin to cook, add the fish sauce, pepper and sugar and stir to blend them with the egg.

Then quickly add the fried aubergine rings and the spring onions, covering them with the scrambled egg. Allow to cook to the consistency of a Spanish omelette. When browned on the underside, turn over and cook the other side.

Transfer to a dish and serve.

OP JUMNEE JRUK BAMPORNG
SWEET-AND-SOUR SPARE RIBS

INGREDIENTS

- 275g (10oz) pork spare ribs from a young pig, chopped into 2.5cm (1in) lengths
- Salt and pepper to taste
- 4 tablespoons oil
- 115g (4oz) fresh pineapple segments
- 2 medium tomatoes, cut into wedges
- 2 large spring onions, coarsely chopped
- 2 tablespoons fish sauce
- 1 tablespoon lime juice
- 2 teaspoons sugar
- 2 tablespoons chicken stock or plain water
- A grinding of black pepper
- Coriander leaves to garnish

PREPARATION

Coat the spare ribs with salt and pepper. Heat the oil in a wok or deep frying pan and fry the spare ribs until golden brown on all sides. Remove from the oil and set aside.

Place the pineapple, tomatoes and spring onions in the hot oil, stir briefly, then add all the remaining ingredients except the coriander. Stir briefly and pour over the spare ribs,

Garnish with coriander leaves and serve.

SAJ GO TIK PRAHOK

BEEF AND RAW VEGETABLES WITH PICKLED FISH DIP

INGREDIENTS

- Tik Prahok (see page 94)
- A selection of raw vegetables, such as longbean, green aubergine, white cabbage and plantain banana
- 225g (8oz) good-quality beef steak
- A piece of pork fat or a cube of lard

This is a dish that I ate at the Hang Neak Restaurant on the banks of the Mekong, while the wedding party was under way. The Cambodians use a special piece of equipment on which the beef is seared, which is not unlike an upturned colander placed over a charcoal grill. It would be possible to improvise something like this over a barbecue, but one of those thick French griddle plates will achieve much the same effect.

PREPARATION

First prepare a bowl of Tik Prahok (see page 94).

Wash and prepare the vegetables according to type: quarter the round aubergines, break up the cabbage into leaves, peel and dice the plantain, etc. Arrange on a serving dish and set aside. Slice the beef into thin slivers.

Preheat a Cambodian grill or a griddle plate. Draw a piece of pork fat or a cube of lard over the cooking surface. When it sizzles, lay strips of beef all over the surface and cook, turning once.

When cooked to taste, lift away, dip into the Tik Prahok sauce and eat with the raw vegetables.

Alternatively, place the whole piece of steak under a very hot grill and sear one side. Turn, sear the other side. Remove, slice thinly and serve.

PLEA SAJ GO

HOT-AND-SOUR BEEF SALAD

INGREDIENTS

- Enough Lettuce leaves to cover a serving dish
- 225g (8oz) tender beef steak
- 2 tablespoons fish sauce
- 2 tablespoons lime juice
- 1 teaspoon sugar
- 1 onion, halved and sliced
- 4–5 small fresh red or green chillies, finely chopped
- 20 chilli leaves (these are hard to find outside Asia; the same amount of mint leaves may be substituted)

PREPARATION

Cover a serving dish with washed and dried lettuce leaves and set aside.

Grill the steak to taste – for authenticity you should leave it very rare. As you grill it, catch the juices in a dish. Quickly slice the steak very thinly, again retaining any juices.

Put the steak and all the juices into a mixing bowl, add the fish sauce and lime juice and mix well. Add all the other ingredients in turn, stirring once between each addition.

After adding the chilli or mint leaves, turn quickly out on the lettuce and serve while still warm.

MUAN CHAR KREUNG

CHICKEN FRIED WITH CURRY PASTE

INGREDIENTS

- 2 tablespoons oil
- 225g (8oz) thinly sliced chicken pieces
- 1 tablespoon prepared curry paste
- 2 tablespoon fish sauce
- 1 teaspoon sugar
- 1 tablespoon ground roasted peanuts
- 1 medium sweet pepper, cut into thin strips

FOR THE CURRY PASTE:

- 2.5cm (1in) piece of galangal, peeled and finely chopped
- 1 tablespoon finely chopped lemon grass
- 1 teaspoon lime rind, finely chopped
- 5 large dried red chillies, soaked in water for 30 minutes, then split open, deseeded and finely chopped
- 1 teaspoon salt

This is another dish from the Samapheap Restaurant near Angkor Wat. The curry paste that you will make for this recipe is also needed for the dish Aamoh on page 101, so you may wish to make double the amount. It will keep in a refrigerator for at least a week.

PREPARATION

First make the curry paste: in a mortar, pound all the ingredients together to form a paste. Set aside.

In a wok or deep frying pan, heat the oil. Add the chicken pieces, stir and add the curry paste. Stir well, then add the other ingredients in succession, stirring once between each addition.

The sweet pepper should barely be in the oil for a moment before you turn everything out on a dish to serve.

MUAN CHAR KHYEY

CHICKEN WITH GINGER

INGREDIENTS

- 2 tablespoons oil
- 225g (8oz) chicken, thinly sliced
- 2 tablespoons oyster sauce
- 5cm (2in) piece of ginger, peeled and cut into fine matchsticks
- 1 teaspoon sugar
- 3 medium spring onions, chopped into 2.5cm (1in) lengths
- A sprinkling of ground black pepper
- 2–3 tablespoons chicken stock (see page 14) or plain water

PREPARATION

In a wok or deep frying pan, heat the oil and briefly fry the chicken, adding the oyster sauce and turning to coat well.

Add all the other ingredients except the stock, stirring constantly. If the mixture appears too dry, add a little chicken stock or water occasionally.

As soon as the chicken is cooked through, remove from the heat and serve.

BAI DAMNERB GRUOP KHANO
GRILLED STICKY RICE WITH COCONUT AND JACKFRUIT

INGREDIENTS

- 1 banana leaf
- 275g (10oz) cooked sticky rice, preferably still warm
- 225ml (8fl oz) coconut milk
- 2 tablespoons sugar
- ½ teaspoon salt
- 60g (2oz) coconut scrapings
- 115g (4oz) jackfruit, coarsely chopped into small pieces
- Toothpicks

This delicious pudding, which I found at Koki Beach, outside Phnom Penh, needs to be grilled inside banana leaf. While this can now be found in the West, you will probably have to buy more than you need here, so look around this book for other recipes that need some. Fresh jackfruit are unlikely to be easily available in the West but tinned segments would do here.

PREPARATION

First cut the banana leaf down either side of the central stem. Discard the stem, set aside one half of the leaf and cut the other into 8 strips, roughly 10cm (4in) wide. Set aside.

In a large bowl, mix the sticky rice with the coconut milk, sugar and salt. Leave to cool and dry (in a cool climate this should take no more than 30 minutes). Roll this mixture into 8 balls and place one on each section of banana leaf. Add to each an equal amount of coconut scrapings and jackfruit. Fold over 2 opposite corners of the leaf section, then fold the 2 remaining corners and pin with a toothpick to make a sealed envelope.

Preheat a moderate grill. Place the 8 envelopes under the grill and cook, turning from time to time, until the leaf envelopes begin to blacken.

Remove, open each envelope and serve the grilled rice balls with jackfruit on the open leaf, either hot or cold (see the photograph on page 105).

MEE CHAR
VEGETARIAN EGG NOODLES

INGREDIENTS

- 2 tablespoons oil
- 2 small garlic cloves, finely chopped
- 1–2 small dried red chillies, coarsely chopped
- 85g (3oz) or 1 nest of egg noodles (see page 11), soaked if dried
- 1 tablespoon dark soy sauce
- 1 tablespoon light soy sauce
- ½ teaspoon sugar
- 60g (2oz) beansprouts
- 60g (2oz) broccoli, cut small
- 60g (2oz) carrot, cut into fine matchsticks
- Coriander leaves to garnish

Those vegetarians who do not eat eggs need not worry: egg noodles are no longer what they were – the yellow colour comes from vegetable dye. If the name still causes concern, however, simply substitute some other white noodle.

PREPARATION

In a wok or deep frying pan, heat the oil and fry the garlic until golden brown. Add the chillies and stir well. Next, add all the remaining ingredients in succession except the coriander, stirring once between each addition.

Mix well, turn out on a serving dish and garnish with the roughly separated coriander leaves.

Vietnam

Mask seller, Hanoi

bombarded and occupied in turn by the French, the Viet Cong and the Americans, leaving only a fraction of its cultural treasures intact.

The hotel is on the bank of the river, where the new or 'European' town was built, while on the opposite side are the remains of the Purple Forbidden City, the walled and moated enclosure that was the private domain of the Imperial family. This was modelled on the Forbidden City in Beijing, and had the same series of interlinked courtyards and pavilions reserved for the Emperor, his Empress and his mother, with only a few buildings, such as the throne hall, accessible to ambassadors from the outside world. Most of the palaces and halls were utterly destroyed in 1968 in the aftermath of the Tet Offensive, when the American and South Vietnamese forces attempted to dislodge the Viet Cong who had carried out a horrendous blood bath after occupying the city. Today, UNESCO is gradually restoring the buildings with great care, starting with the outer gate-houses, so that it is possible to see something of the sumptuous red and gold carvings, the gilded furnishings and the jade and silver ornaments that lay hidden behind the high blank walls and which must once have rivalled their original inspiration in China.

The last Imperial family, the Nguyen dynasty, only came to power as late as 1802 and had hardly unified the country before the French began to meddle in their affairs. To see something of their brief rule one must recross the river and travel out to the hills beyond the new town, to where each succeeding Emperor built himself a fabulous tomb in order to ensure his worship and thus his repose for eternity. All the tombs are different and the most highly regarded are those that display a subtle integration of buildings and landscape, with walkways and terraces interlaced with lakes and pagodas. I have to admit, however, to liking best the one that the experts most denigrate, the slightly bizarre concrete

construction put up by the Emperor Khai Dinh, who ruled from 1916 to 1925, but who spent a good deal of time enjoying himself in France. This is reflected in the main hall of his mortuary complex, which looks surprisingly like a casino from Nice or Monte Carlo. But this strange exterior is as nothing to the surprise within. You enter in darkness, someone trips a switch and suddenly, under arc lights, you see the larger-than-life gilded bronze statue of Khai Dinh himself, seated on his throne, sternly gazing over the hills to some distant point – perhaps a favourite restaurant in Cannes!

In Hué itself I was able to combine culture and food as it was only a short cyclo ride from the Purple Forbidden City along the river bank to the main market, one of the largest in the country. The evident abundance of all the regular Southeast Asian produce was a sign that the country is undergoing a rebirth of private enterprise, with stalls selling ducks and pigs. These were once rarities but are now seen everywhere, and I was told that demand for such delicacies is insatiable. That and the number of shaky trucks pounding along the main roads, exacerbating the already hair-raising traffic, are the best testimony to the restoration of the private distribution system.

There are two other aspects of a Vietnamese market that stand out: first the extraordinarily large snails that you see in buckets and heaps everywhere. I never found them on any menu, though I was told they are a popular staple, stuffed and cooked with pork and herbs. Being about the size of tennis balls, they were clearly a useful foodstuff. I was, however, less happy about the other notable product on sale in Hué and elsewhere – dog. I can eat most things, but being a dog-lover this is too much for me. I had seen dogs in China, in Canton, but they had been alive in cages, waiting for a buyer – bad enough, but nothing compared to the area in most Vietnamese markets where you find a butcher's slab with dog's heads, dog steaks and, yes, dog sausages! I turned and fled, but it gave me bad dreams.

Fortunately my hotel had an excellent restaurant, the Riverside Café, which specialized in classic Vietnamese cookery as well as local delicacies like deep-fried quail, steamed fish with vegetables, and crab claws wrapped in prawn and shrimp, several of which I have included here. Overall, Hué was my best experience for fine food. This was undoubtedly due to a phenomenon I'd witnessed in China, where the new Western-built hotels have brought in top chefs from Hong Kong and Singapore who are beginning to revive the forgotten glories of Chinese cuisine in its native land. For similar reasons the An Phu restaurant, not far from the hotel at 14b Chu Van An, was worth a visit because it too is locked into the tourist trade and has raised standards that are elsewhere abysmally low. One hears much about the destructive effects of global tourism, but in terms of food and restaurants the effects are often highly beneficial in places where the old traditions have nearly died out.

**Farmers carrying
straw near Song Can**

I did find one hardy survivor – a little food stall near the point where the Perfume River branches off into the Nhug River, forming a small lake where fishermen bang the sides of their boats to drive the shoals of freshwater fish into nets stretched on poles across the water. Drawn to the sound of this drumming, I saw a small shop-house on the river bank, where a woman was squatting at a charcoal brazier, patiently making complicated pancakes. These turned out to be the most delicious things I ate during my entire visit – a crispy rice flour base filled with pork, shrimp and beansprouts with a touch of egg, served with a dipping sauce heavily flavoured with mint. The surroundings were less than salubrious. Stacked tins of motor oil suggested that the primary function of the business was car maintenance, though I've eaten in worse places and it hardly detracted from the pleasure of watching the deft way in which the woman produced these delicate morsels.

Feeling a lot better about Vietnam, I headed for the coast and the pleasant drive over the mountains to the port of Danang. This had been at the centre of American military activity, famous as a 'rest and recreation centre' where GIs relaxed before returning to the front line. Having suffered terribly at the hands of rioting South Vietnamese troops, followed by vengeful North Vietnamese occupiers, the city is now struggling to recapture some of its former zest. Superbly situated on a promontory where the Han River flows into the Bay of Danang and thence on to the South China Sea, the port is already bustling with ocean-going vessels as business revives. So much so that there was no room in the Marco Polo, the best hotel in town, which set me on a long and increasingly frantic search for a decent place to stay. Eventually I discovered a brand new block and found myself inside the just-opened, and hopefully named, Modern Hotel where the owners' enthusiasm made up for what they lacked in experience. Better

still, the hotel was right on Bach Dang Street, which runs along the river beside the main port area, near to most of the town's sights and activities.

It was only a short walk to the Cho Han market, a rather gloomy covered arcade that spills out into the surrounding streets and which gave me an even wider view of what Vietnam has to offer. Happily, the Cho Han is a vegetable market, so there was no dog stall in evidence, but what struck me most were the little shops in the surrounding streets that specialize in cooking equipment, most of it locally made. Here it is clear that, despite the surface crudeness – hand-forged scissors, heavy knives and axes, charcoal stoves cannibalized from old tins – Vietnam has managed to develop a simple technological base. There was also evidence of a considerable amount of canning, bottling and packaging of preserved and dried ingredients, from the well-known nuoc nam fish sauce that is exported world wide, down to neat little packets of spices with brightly coloured pop-art graphics, a treasure trove for collectors of naive art.

The most telling sign of economic growth is Danang's rush-hour scramble, with countless bicycles pouring down every road. When this coincides with the end of the school day, you are treated to the extraordinary spectacle of hundreds of pretty Vietnamese girls riding home, all wearing the traditional au dai, the long white jacket split at the sides that manages to be simultaneously modest and revealing, and which is usually topped off with a traditional white shell hat. Some individualistic souls try to vary this with a woolly pom-pom hat or a straw bonnet with artificial flowers, but whatever they wear, everyone smiles.

After bicycling girls, the next best thing in Danang is the Cham Museum. Originally set up by the French, this houses the stunning collection of sculpture found on local excavations, much of it heavily influenced by Indian originals with statues of Shiva, Brahma and Vishnu. That aside, little of the French era has survived. The only person who tried to speak the language to me was the old guardian of the Catholic Cathedral, who was touchingly eager for me to admire the stained glass windows and plaster saints, all of which had been 'Made in France'.

Memories of the American era are evoked by a trip to the once-famous China Beach, subject of many pop songs, where the GIs used to relax between missions. On the way out of town I noticed a building surrounded by wooden frames, on which strands of yellow egg noodles were drying. Stopping the taxi, I went in to find a real old-fashioned noodle factory, where a huge stone wheel was squeezing the dough before it passed through a second machine that separated it into long strands. I did not, however, see any eggs, confirming what I had long suspected, that most egg noodle in Asia is made with artificial colouring – good news for vegetarians, if nothing else! Indeed, any vegetarians are well covered in Danang as there are several purely vegetarian eating places around the Cho Han market, though they follow the

**An old lady about
to enjoy her meal**

Chinese practice of serving up non-meat meals dressed to look like meat – beancurd rabbits or chickens made out of mushrooms – so you don't feel you're missing anything.

My last full day in Vietnam was the high spot of the visit: a drive out to the coastal town of Hoi An, an old Chinese trading post that is surely one of the prettiest places in Asia. It was to Hoi An that the Chinese junks came, from the seventeenth century onwards, joined later by sailors from Holland, Portugal and Japan. After crossing the pretty little 'Japanese Covered Bridge', the visitor can stroll down a delightful main street, past handsome teakwood merchants houses and the sumptuously decorated temples and pagodas that were built by the various sailors' guilds, whose members endowed them with sculptures and furnishings brought from a homeland that many of them would never see again. Best of all are the houses themselves, some of them dating back to the eighteenth century, whose dark salons are furnished with lacquered tables and chairs inlaid with mother-of-pearl, the walls hung with long-robed ancestor paintings under glass, silk hangings and tall vases decorated with wispy reeds and wading herons. Each salon leads out into a brightly lit courtyard, then on to another set of rooms, ending in a kitchen, beyond which is a tiny walled garden. It is a vision of an ideal Chinese home, born of nostalgia and almost impossible to find in China itself.

In a tangible way, Hoi An sets Vietnamese history in context, revealing its 'other', Chinese side, the element that makes it subtly different from its neighbours in Southeast Asia. The kitchens in these Sino-Vietnamese mansions are living museums of the country's culinary history. In the rest of the region, cooking takes place at ground level on a charcoal burner, but in Hoi An you find

Rush hour, Danang

a high, waist-level brick platform with two openings, one for a wok, the other for a steamer, under which are the fires. There is a side table for preparation, and outside in the yard stand large earthenware water jars. The room itself is blackened and scented with the age-old aromas of cooking.

Back in Danang that night I was again treated to one of those sudden swings between heaven and hell that seems to characterize a country in transition – I managed to find a restaurant that had no food to sell, none at all! The Modern Hotel did manage to save the day by coming up with a Vietnamese clay pot of meat and vegetables, even if the plastic spoon was starting to melt in the hot stock! The return journey the following day also brought out some of the things that still make Vietnam difficult for visitors: the long wait for a connection at Hanoi airport, with nothing to eat except sticky approximations of French pâtisserie, followed by endless queues past officials who clearly hadn't learned how to work their computer terminals, though at least my worries about having the wrong documents proved groundless.

Overall it had been a fascinating trip, though I would advise anyone who wants to see the country to take an organized tour; the individual traveller is forced to waste a good deal of time just arranging quite simple things. South Vietnam has already established international standard hotels with first-class food and, if things go on as they are, the rest of the country should follow. For the present, a visit is still something of an adventure, but with Hué and Hoi An in mind, one that is well worth the effort.

BANH KHOAI
VIETNAMESE SAVOURY PANCAKE

INGREDIENTS

- 115g (4oz) rice flour
- 1 teaspoon ground turmeric
- ½ teaspoon salt
- 3 tablespoons oil
- 2 garlic cloves, finely chopped
- 60g (2oz) minced pork
- 60g (2oz) pork fillet, thinly sliced
- 60g (2oz) small shrimps
- 60g (2oz) beansprouts
- 60g (2oz) onion, finely chopped
- 1 teaspoon sugar
- 1 tablespoon fish sauce
- ¼ teaspoon ground white pepper
- 1 egg

FOR THE SAUCE:

- 60g (2oz) cucumber, chopped into small dice
- 60g (2oz) carrot, chopped into small dice
- 60g (2oz) onion, chopped into small dice
- 2 large fresh red or green chillies, finely chopped
- 20 mint leaves, coarsely chopped
- 2 tablespoons fish sauce
- 1 teaspoon sugar
- 2 tablespoons rice vinegar or white wine vinegar

This was the pancake I watched being made in Hué and it was probably the tastiest thing I ate in Vietnam.

PREPARATION

First make the sauce: mix all the ingredients together and set aside.

In a bowl, mix the flour, turmeric and salt with 450ml (¾ pint) water to make a smooth batter. Set aside.

Heat 2 tablespoons of the oil in a wok or deep frying pan and stir-fry all the remaining ingredients except the egg in succession, stirring after each addition. Check that the pork slices are just cooked through, then remove from the heat and set aside.

Break the egg into a bowl, beat it lightly and set aside.

Place a flat-bottomed 20cm (8in) crêpe or omelette pan on a high heat. Pour in a little oil (no more than 1 tablespoon), spread it evenly with a spatula and pour off any excess. Stir the batter, then pour in just enough to coat the bottom of the pan.

Using a spatula to check when the underside of this pancake is almost cooked, place a little mound of the stir-fried ingredients on one half of the pancake, just off centre. Drip about 1 tablespoon of the beaten egg over this, then lift the opposite corner of the pancake over the filled half. Press down lightly, leave to cook briefly, then lift out of the pan and serve at once. Repeat the procedure until all the batter and/or the stuffing is used up.

Serve the pancakes with the sauce.

BO XAO MANG
BEEF WITH BAMBOO SHOOTS

INGREDIENTS

- 2 tablespoons sesame oil
- 225g (8oz) beef steak, thinly sliced
- 115g (4oz) bamboo shoots, thinly sliced
- 1 tablespoon fish sauce
- ½ teaspoon sugar
- 1 large fresh red chilli, finely chopped
- 2 spring onions, chopped into 2.5cm (1in) lengths
- 1 teaspoon white sesame seeds

PREPARATION

Heat the oil and briefly stir-fry the beef until just cooked through.

Add all the remaining ingredients in turn, stirring between each addition.

As soon as the sesame seeds are stirred in, remove from the heat, turn out on a plate and serve.

MI XAO DA NANG

DANANG FRIED NOODLE

INGREDIENTS

- 2 tablespoons oil
- 60g (2oz) onions, coarsely chopped
- 115g (4oz) beef steak, thinly sliced
- 115g (4oz) egg noodles, soaked if dried
- 60g (2oz) black fungus mushroom, coarsely chopped (see page 19)
- 60g (2oz) celery, coarsely chopped
- 60g (2oz) tomatoes, coarsely chopped
- 1 tablespoon fish sauce
- 1 tablespoon light soy sauce
- 1 tablespoon sugar
- ¼ teaspoon ground white pepper
- Coriander leaves to garnish

This is a dish prepared with the yellow noodles I saw being made on the road to China Beach outside Danang. I've suggested using beef here; but, as with most noodle dishes, you could substitute pork, chicken, seafood, or even a firm vegetable like mushrooms or broccoli, as required.

PREPARATION

Heat the oil in a wok or deep frying pan and fry the onions briefly. Add the beef and stir-fry until almost cooked through.

Add all the remaining ingredients except the coriander in succession, stirring between each addition.

As soon as the ground pepper is stirred in, turn the mixture out on a plate, garnish with the coriander and serve.

PHO GA HANH XAO

CHICKEN NOODLE SOUP WITH CRISPY SHALLOTS

INGREDIENTS

- 2 tablespoons oil
- 2 small red shallots, finely chopped
- 450ml (¾ pint) chicken stock (see page 14)
- 60g (2oz) beansprouts
- 115g (4oz) medium flat rice flour noodles (see page 11), soaked if dried
- 85g (3oz) boneless chicken, thinly sliced
- 1 tablespoon fish sauce
- 1 tablespoon light soy sauce
- ½ teaspoon sugar
- 1 spring onion, finely chopped

This is the classic Vietnamese noodle dish in which the use of shallot and fish sauce clearly show how different the country's cuisine is from that of China. It is a wonderfully comforting dish for a wet or cold day.

PREPARATION

Heat the oil in a wok and fry the shallots until golden brown. Remove from the heat and reserve both the oil and the shallots together.

Heat the stock in a pan and simmer until required.

Bring a pan of water to the boil. Using a mesh ladle strainer, dip the beansprouts in the water to blanch them for 10 seconds. Remove, shake to drain well and place in a large serving bowl. Repeat the process with the noodles, blanching them for 20 seconds, then the chicken, again for 20 seconds.

Add the fish and soy sauces to the bowl with the sugar. Stir well. Pour the hot stock into the bowl and stir. Sprinkle with the chopped spring onion, then pour over about half of the oil and shallots.

Serve, with the remaining oil and shallots in a side dish for diners to use as required.

BUN THIT HEO NUONG
GRILLED PORK WITH RICE VERMICELLI

INGREDIENTS
- 225g (8oz) pork, thinly sliced

FOR THE MARINADE:
- 1 stalk of lemon grass, finely chopped then pounded
- 2 garlic cloves, finely chopped then pounded
- 5 small red shallots, finely chopped then pounded
- 2 tablespoons fish sauce
- 1 teaspoon sugar
- ½ teaspoon ground white pepper
- 1 tablespoon sesame oil
- 1 teaspoon white sesame seeds

FOR THE SAUCE:
- 2 tablespoons fish sauce
- 1 tablespoon rice vinegar
- 1 teaspoon sugar
- 1 garlic clove, finely chopped
- 2 small fresh red or green chillies, finely chopped

FOR THE NOODLES:
- 115g (4oz) rice vermicelli (see page 11)
- 60g (2oz) beansprouts
- 20 sweet basil leaves

While this can be served as a main course, it also makes a very satisfying one-dish meal.

PREPARATION

In a bowl, mix all the marinade ingredients. Place the sliced pork in the bowl and turn to coat thoroughly. Leave to marinate for 30 minutes.

While the pork is marinating, make the sauce: mix all the ingredients thoroughly with 1 tablespoon water and turn into a serving bowl.

Preheat a moderate grill.

Make the noodles: heat a large pan of water. When boiling, place the vermicelli in a long-handled strainer and plunge into the pan briefly. Remove, drain and turn out on a large serving platter. Arrange the raw beansprouts and sweet basil leaves to one side of the bed of noodles.

Grill the marinated pork until golden brown on both sides: this should only take a minute. Remove, place on a separate dish and serve with the vermicelli and the sauce.

Diners should take some vermicelli and some beansprouts and basil leaves on their plate and pour over a little sauce, then put some grilled pork beside the mixture.

THAN CHAN CHANH
KIDNEYS WITH MINT AND LIME

INGREDIENTS
- 2 pigs' kidneys, thinly sliced to keep the distinct 'comma' outline of the kidney
- 115g (4oz) onion, finely chopped
- 1 tablespoon finely chopped ginger
- 2 tablespoons lime juice
- ¼ teaspoon ground black pepper
- ¼ teaspoon salt
- 20 mint leaves

Many people today are resistant to kidneys because of the strong flavour, which is often disguised by thick sauces. This recipe is remarkable because the Vietnamese love of fresh citrus flavours removes any trace of unpleasantness, resulting in a dish which is surprisingly sharp and fresh.

PREPARATION

Bring a pan of water to the boil. Put in the sliced kidney and blanch for 1 minute. Remove and drain.

Place in a large bowl and add all the other ingredients. Stir well, turn out on a plate and serve.

NEM CUON SONG

FRESH 'NEM' SPRING ROLL

INGREDIENTS

- 115g (4oz) lean pork
- 60g (2oz) rice vermicelli (see page 11)
- 115g (4oz) small shrimps
- 60g (2oz) beansprouts
- 3 tablespoons ground peanuts
- 2 tablespoons coarsely chopped coriander leaves
- 12 sheets of banh trang rice paper (see page 11)

TO SERVE:

- Lettuce leaves
- Mint leaves

FOR THE PHUANG
NAM DIPPING SAUCE:

- 2 tablespoons fish sauce
- 2 tablespoons rice vinegar or white wine vinegar
- 1 tablespoon water
- 1 teaspoon very finely chopped ginger
- 1 teaspoon sugar
- 2 small fresh red or green chillies, finely chopped
- 1 garlic clove, finely chopped

PREPARATION

First make the phuang nam dipping sauce: mix all the ingredients together and serve in individual bowls.

Heat a pan of water and boil the pork until just cooked through. Remove, drain well and chop very finely. Set aside.

Change the water and bring to the boil. Using a mesh ladle strainer, dip the rice vermicelli in the boiling water for about 10 seconds. Remove and plunge into cold water to arrest the cooking. Drain, break up roughly and set aside.

Repeat the blanching procedure with the shrimps, for 5 seconds only. Remove, drain, finely chop and set aside. Repeat with the beansprouts, blanching for 10 seconds only.

Give each diner a plate on which is laid a folded napkin that has been soaked in cold water. Next, arrange the blanched ingredients on a serving platter along with the rice paper sheets and mounds of the ground peanuts and coriander leaves. Place this on the table with the dipping bowls and with another serving platter bearing the lettuce and mint leaves.

To make a nem: take a rice paper sheet and dampen it on a wet napkin. Lay it on a plate and arrange a mix of the blanched ingredients in a line. Sprinkle this filling with the peanuts and coriander. Take the near edge of the sheet and roll it over the filling to form a tube: the dampened paper should stick together, making a manageable roll that can be lifted and dipped in the sauce. This should be eaten with the lettuce and mint leaves.

GOI GA

CHICKEN SALAD WITH MINT AND NUTS

INGREDIENTS

- 175g (6oz) skinless chicken breast fillet
- 85g (3oz) beansprouts
- 85g (3oz) cucumber, cut in half lengthways, deseeded, then cut into fine matchsticks about 5cm (2in) long
- 85g (3oz) onion, finely chopped
- 2 tablespoons fish sauce
- 2 tablespoons lime juice
- 1 tablespoon finely chopped mint leaves
- 2 tablespoons ground roasted peanuts
- 2 teaspoons sesame seeds, dry-fried

This mix of crisp salad heavily flavoured with mint seems to me to be more typical of true Vietnamese cuisine than the meat in thick sauces often served in Vietnamese restaurants in the West.

PREPARATION

Bring a pan of water to the boil, add the chicken breast and simmer until cooked through. Remove and allow to cool.

Shred the meat into small pieces over a bowl, allowing any liquid it may still retain to fall into the bowl. Put all the remaining ingredients into the bowl and stir well. Turn out on a plate and serve.

CANG CUA CHIEN

DEEP-FRIED CRAB CLAWS IN A PORK AND PRAWN ENVELOPE

INGREDIENTS

- 85g (3oz) minced pork
- 115g (4oz) shelled and deveined raw prawns, finely chopped
- 1 egg
- 1 garlic clove, finely chopped
- 1 tablespoon fish sauce
- 1 tablespoon oyster sauce
- 1 teaspoon cornflour
- ¼ teaspoon ground white pepper
- 6–8 crab claws (depending on size)
- Oil for deep-frying

FOR THE PLUM SAUCE:

- 1 whole preserved plum (see page 19)
- 225ml (8fl oz) rice vinegar or white wine vinegar
- 5 tablespoons sugar

I liked this so much when I tried it at Hué's Riverside Café, not only for its rich mix of flavours but also because it looks so good. It makes a dramatic dinner-party offering.

PREPARATION

First make the plum sauce: with a fork, shred the flesh of the plum from its stone – this should leave you with tiny scrapings. Set aside. Place the vinegar and sugar in a saucepan and heat to make a syrup. Stir in the plum scrapings, turn into a dipping dish and set aside.

In a bowl, thoroughly mix all the remaining ingredients except the crab claws and oil. Divide the mixture by the number of crab claws (6–8) and mould a piece round the meaty section at the end of each claw, leaving the pincer itself exposed.

Preheat the oil and deep-fry the coated crab claws until the moulded envelopes are a deep golden brown. Remove, drain and serve with the plum sauce.

CHA GIO CHAY

VEGETARIAN FRIED SPRING ROLL

INGREDIENTS

- 115g (4oz) cellophane noodles, soaked (see page 11)
- 30g (1oz) black fungus mushroom, finely chopped (see page 19)
- 60g (2oz) carrot, grated
- 60g (2oz) white cabbage, grated
- 1 tablespoon light soy sauce
- 1 garlic clove, finely chopped
- 1 tablespoon ground roasted peanuts
- ¼ teaspoon ground white pepper
- 1 teaspoon sugar
- 15 sheets of banh trang rice paper (see page 11)
- Oil for deep-frying

TO SERVE:

- Phuang nam dipping sauce (page 122)
- Lettuce leaves
- Mint leaves

PREPARATION

Drain the noodles, coarsely chop and place in a bowl. Add all the vegetables, soy sauce, garlic, peanuts, pepper and sugar. Mix well.

Fill a flat soup bowl with hot water and drag each rice paper sheet through it to soften. Lay the damp sheets on a board and place a line of the noodle mixture across each. Take up an edge parallel to the line and roll the sheet into a tube. When you reach the centre tuck in a little of the outside edges then continue rolling until the tube is complete – the dampened paper should stick together. There will be approximately 60 spring rolls.

When all the rolls are complete, heat the oil and deep-fry the rolls in batches of 3–4, until golden brown. Remove, drain and keep warm, uncovered, until all are done.

Cut each roll into 4 pieces, then serve with the phuang nam dipping sauce and lettuce and mint leaves.

CA HAP NAM
STEAMED FISH WITH MUSHROOMS

INGREDIENTS
- 1 whole small sea bass (or similar firm fish)
- 2 garlic cloves, thinly sliced
- 60g (2oz) button mushrooms, thinly sliced
- 60g (2oz) black fungus mushroom, soaked, drained then thinly sliced (see page 19)
- 60g (2oz) carrots, finely chopped
- 60g (2oz) onion, finely chopped
- 2 tablespoons light soy sauce
- ½ teaspoon sugar
- ¼ teaspoon ground white pepper
- A grating of nutmeg

This is my version of the steamed fish with vegetables that I ate at the Riverside Café in Hué. I've simplified the number of vegetables, making it mainly a mushroom dish. You could add more.

PREPARATION
Place the sea bass on an oval plate that will fit into the upper compartment of a steamer. Place all the remaining ingredients on top of the fish, spreading them evenly. Place the dish in the steamer and cook until the fish is just cooked through, about 15 minutes, depending on size. Remove from the steamer, dab away any water from the dish with kitchen paper, then serve.

CHIM CUOC CHIEN
DEEP-FRIED QUAIL

INGREDIENTS
- 1 teaspoon coriander seeds
- 3 garlic cloves
- ½ teaspoon black peppercorns
- 1 stalk of lemon grass, coarsely chopped
- 4 quails
- 2 tablespoons light soy sauce
- 2 teaspoons honey
- Oil for deep-frying
- Lime Dip (see page 129), to serve

PREPARATION
In a mortar, pound the coriander seeds, garlic cloves, peppercorns and lemon grass to make a paste. Spread this over the quails, then sprinkle the birds with soy sauce. Spoon over the honey and leave to marinate for 1 hour. When ready to cook, heat the oil for deep-frying and cook the quail until golden brown (you could also barbecue them). Serve with the lime dip.

NOM DU DU THIT BO NUONG
GRILLED BEEF WITH RAW PAPAYA

INGREDIENTS
- 115g (4oz) lean beef steak
- 85g (3oz) green raw papaya, grated or slivered
- 60g (2oz) carrot, grated or slivered, as above
- 4 small fresh red or green chillies, finely chopped
- 1 tablespoon fish sauce
- 1 tablespoon lime juice
- ½ teaspoon sugar
- 1 tablespoon ground roasted peanuts
- 10 mint leaves

This dish seemed to be especially popular in the port of Danang, to judge by the number of food sellers cooking it on portable stoves. It is one of those dishes that the diner can adjust to taste by adding more fish sauce and lime juice as required. I've given a minimum amount here, but you could put out little bowls of these flavours for diners to take if they wish.

PREPARATION
Grill the steak to taste, then thinly slice it and place in a serving bowl. Add all the other ingredients and mix thoroughly. Turn out on a dish and serve.

BANH CHUOI
BANANA AND SWEET POTATO FRITTERS

INGREDIENTS
- 115g (4oz) rice flour
- 225ml (8fl oz) coconut milk
- ½ teaspoon salt
- 60g (2oz) sugar
- 5 small or 2 large unripe bananas (the skins just turning yellow)
- 1 medium sweet potato
- Oil for deep-frying

This is the delicacy that the street vendor was making near my hotel in Hanoi and was the first thing I ate in Vietnam. Banana fritters are sold all over Southeast Asia, but this combination with sweet potato is especially good. The street seller in Hanoi had a neat way of frying this while measuring out a portion for sale – she used a flat 'shovel' spatula on which she arranged 2 slices of banana, then in the opposite direction, 2 slices of sweet potato. She dipped the loaded shovel into the hot oil, lifted it out and slipped the golden fritters into a twist of paper.

PREPARATION
Mix the flour, coconut milk, salt and sugar to a smooth mixture and set aside. Cut the small bananas in half or the long bananas into 3 pieces each. This should give pieces about 7.5cm (3in) long. Cut these pieces lengthways into strips about 1cm (½in) thick. Do the same thing with the sweet potato: cut it in half, then cut the halves into thin strips.

Preheat the oil for deep-frying. Dip the strips in the batter, shake off any excess and place them in the hot oil. Fry until golden brown, remove, drain and serve immediately.

CHA CA NAM
GRILLED FISH WITH MUSHROOM SAUCE

INGREDIENTS
- 4 tablespoons sesame oil
- 1 small whole firm-fleshed fish (such as trout)
- 5 small red shallots, coarsely chopped
- 115g (4oz) dried Chinese mushrooms, soaked, drained then thinly sliced (see page 19)
- 1 tablespoon fish sauce
- 1 tablespoon light soy sauce
- ½ teaspoon cornflour
- 3 spring onions, cut into 2.5cm (1in) lengths
- ¼ teaspoon ground white pepper

PREPARATION
Pour 2 tablespoons of the sesame oil over the fish, coat well and leave for 15 minutes. Preheat a moderate grill. In the meantime, heat the remaining oil and fry the shallots until crispy and golden. Remove and set aside, retaining the oil. Grill the fish until just cooked through. Using your fingers, break up the fish into chunks, carefully removing any bones. Place the fish pieces on a serving dish and set aside. Reheat the reserved oil and stir-fry the mushrooms briefly. Add the fish sauce and the light soy sauce and stir. Mix the cornflour with 3 tablespoons water and add just enough of this mixture to thicken the liquid in the pan slightly. Add the spring onions and the ground white pepper and stir once. Remove from the heat and pour over the fish. Scatter the crispy fried shallots on top and serve.

Burma

BE NICE TO NATS

On my first night in Burma I was invited to eat with some friends at their home in Golden Valley Road, in the garden suburb just beyond the main commercial centre of the city the British called Rangoon, but which to its inhabitants has always been Yangon. Many things about that evening revealed aspects of the current situation in the country. Burma is supposed to have undergone a prolonged revolutionary experience, shut off from the outside world, yet here was an old, well-placed family in Western clothes, giving a dinner party in the sort of smart detached house with front porch and bay windows that you might find in a quiet English suburb. There were comfortable armchairs and servants in the traditional wrap-around longyis, offering whisky and soda or gin and tonic before the meal. Somehow this family of professional people — diplomats, doctors and teachers, with a sprinkling of businessmen and women — had survived the upheavals since the country's independence in 1948 and the subsequent years of military rule, keeping their way of life reasonably intact.

That night there was talk of the future, of hopes that Burma would rejoin the outside world at last, that the economy would improve and democracy flourish. Of course there were fears, too. Only a short walk away was the compound where Aung San Suu Kyi was living under house-arrest since her victory in the national elections that were annulled by the grimly named SLORC (the State Law and Restoration Council). This was 1995 and since then Aung San Suu Kyi has called for a tourist boycott. Some opposition leaders do not agree with her and wish the country to remain open to visitors, so individual travellers will have to decide for themselves. In a sense this means that little has changed. For much of the period since the British handed over power, tourism was discouraged and only 24-hour visas were issued. An extension to seven days didn't alter much, as it was still impossible to see the country's main historical sites in so limited a time. This was why so many Thais, myself included, had never visited one of our closest neighbours. It was the recent decision to grant full visas that encouraged me to fly on to Rangoon after my visit to Vietnam, a swing to the opposite pole of Southeast Asia's cultural pendulum — from France and China to Britain and India.

In Rangoon it is the Britishness you see first — the imposing Imperial buildings, with their mix of Classical and Gothic, the aston-

Protection from the sun with a powder made from Thanaka bark

ishing number of parks, gardens and flower beds that are the great legacy of the British municipal tradition. Even my hotel was set in its own grounds and, although now called Best Executive Suites, was once a set of bungalows used by young unmarried officers out from Britain to administer this distant colonial outpost. Each bungalow still has its own servant, who potters around, mothering her charges, cooking a full English breakfast of bacon and eggs with toast and marmalade, served under the cooling draught of the revolving ceiling fans.

The British chose to call the country Burma, though historically this has always been its informal name, the formal title being Myanmar — rather like The Netherlands (formal) and Holland (informal). SLORC has proposed reversing the British choice by calling the country Myanmar and using more local versions of place names such as Yangon for Rangoon, but until this is confirmed by a properly elected government the outside world will no doubt wish to apply a policy of 'wait-and-see'.

The word Burma is derived from the Bamars, the country's largest ethnic group, who occupy the central area along the River Irrawaddy, from Rangoon up to Pagan and on to the old capital of Mandalay. While this is all most visitors can hope to see, it is as well to bear in mind that there are some 67 ethnic groups that make up Burma's extraordinarily diverse population. These include the Paduang 'Giraffe Women', their necks stretched by up to 25cm (10in) by the copper and brass necklaces that tribal tradition expects them to wear. There are also some groups, like the Shan and the Karen, still fighting for independence from what they see as Bamar dominance.

Apart from the change of names, one of the main effects of British rule was to bring the country closer to its Western neighbour – for a time it was absorbed into the Indian Empire. Even when Burma was separately run, the colonial power continued to import Indian soldiers, administrators and traders. You get a glimpse of this era of the Raj behind the neo-classical façade of Rangoon's Strand Hotel. Despite being recently upgraded to 'international' standard, this still retains much of its old-world charm, with Indian waiters pottering about, serving afternoon tea in shuttered rooms to white-suited figures slumped in club chairs.

Even the city's main emporium, the old Scott Market – now the Bogyoke Aung San Market – a series of cavernous halls, has the air of an Indian bazaar. There are black-market moneychangers and rows of cloth-merchants' stalls stacked high with the wonderful, brightly printed longyis that men and women prefer to wear – at least in the evening when relaxing. There are also signs that this Indian link is not the whole story, that rather like the Chinese aspects of Vietnamese life it was more a result of colonialism than something truly at the heart of the nation's culture. After all, the dominant feature of Rangoon's skyline is the great gilded stupa of the fabulous Shwedagon Pagoda, surrounded by a cluster of prayer halls with their massive statues of the Buddha, guarded by giants and mythical creatures. Everything there, from the richly carved and burnished architecture, to the hosts of saffron-robed monks, is so clearly part of the same heritage that you find in Thailand, Laos and Cambodia.

This sense of another tradition is reinforced by the food section of the market, where one is immediately back in the Southeast Asian world of lemon grass and holy basil, of the pungent aromas of fermented fish and purple shrimp paste and, of course, noodle stalls. At one of these I had to try the only Burmese dish that is known outside its borders – what we Thais call kow soy, but which is known in its homeland as Khauk-swe (see page 153). This is a fiery mix of coriander seeds, turmeric, ginger, chilli and shallots, made palatable with coconut milk and soothing egg noodles, a dish that embodies all those various elements, Indian and Southeast Asian, that I had been so aware of since I arrived.

In the past, much of the public restaurant trade was in the hands of Indian or Chinese business-people and every book I have ever read on Burmese food has made it absolutely clear that it can only be found in Burmese homes. Even today, there are hardly any Burmese restaurants outside the country and those few are likely to be run by Indians who left Burma in the difficult years, just as

Temple courtyard in Pagan

few years back, in order to prepare the site for the huge influx of tourists that has long been announced but slow to happen. Unconsulted and with little time to prepare, the entire population was transported to a new settlement closer to the river, though they still come back to make offerings at the countless shrines and some attempt to plant crops, mainly peanuts, in the dry soil around the sacred buildings.

I stayed in the government-run Thiri Pyitsaya Hotel near the new town, an adequate place, though I was glad that my friends had told me other places where I could eat. After a hard morning's temple visiting, it was good to sit outside under a shady tree at the River View Restaurant, where a truly magnificent khauk-swe was served up, quite different from the simple version I had eaten in the Rangoon Market. This time there were bowls both of chicken soup and fish in coconut sauce, while the noodles and other ingredients – chopped shallots, chilli, pickled cabbage and pickled garlic – were served separately, ready to be mixed as one chose. The result was that I ate too much and what ought to have been a light snack before more hard sightseeing turned into a feast.

What keeps even an overfed visitor going are the constant surprises offered by the truly astonishing buildings. Each ruler seems to have gone to extraordinary lengths to outshine his predecessors, building high and wide and adding ever more audacious embellishments, much of it during the 11th and 12th centuries BC. One temple offers the unusual spectacle of pairs of identical Buddhas seated side by side, presumably on the principle that two of anything are better than one.

Some temples take considerable effort before they yield up their treasures. One involved a ride up the wide and fast-flowing Irrawaddy in a large 'tourist' pleasure boat. This was too big for the few passengers who elected to make the half-hour journey, hugging the eerily empty water's edge with only the occasional two-man rowing boat to vary the scene. There followed a rather laborious walk along the sandy river bank, then a climb up a cliff to a hollow tower inside which was an enormous Buddha, so high one had to bend back almost double to see its face. A solitary hermit monk guards the place and he offered me tea and sweet baby bananas in return for the chance to talk to someone. I couldn't help feeling that his wooden shack must seem very spooky at night, when he is alone amongst all these deserted ruins and silent statues. He did, however, have some source of electricity, judging by the winking fairy lights he had draped around his private shrine at the back of the room. He had also tried to cheer the place up by covering every surface with snapshots sent to him by passing visitors when they returned home.

Even so short a trip along the Irrawaddy was magical. There is now a luxury cruiser which will allow visitors to make the journey from Pagan to Mandalay in some style – private cabins, first-class restaurant, swimming pool – though even the old river steamers have a certain allure, provided you carry your own supplies and have plenty of good books to read.

Back on land, and somewhat satiated with temples, I decided to visit the Pagan market. At the entrance was the betel seller,

A Paduang 'Giraffe Woman'

making up his refreshing snack of folded betel leaf with its filling of bitter paste and chopped betel nut, often taken to aid digestion after a good meal. Just inside the market were the rice merchants seated beside their open sacks. There you can examine the different varieties and qualities of the precious grain – red, white, green, yellow and black, subdivided into those with rough or smooth grain and husk and those that are long or short, round or fat. Few beyond the farmers themselves can detect such subtleties – for most of us there is simply white rice or the more healthy brown variety, and the white can generally be divided into long-grain or short-grain types. Even I, a regular eater of rice, can make do with that. However, for those to whom rice is everything, with all other foodstuffs being little more than flavourings, these varieties are as important as the difference between, say, beef and pork to a meat eater.

Seeing the rice-seller was a forceful reminder that I was no longer among city-dwellers, with their 'international' cooking, and that I was getting closer to 'real' Burmese food. Rice aside, perhaps the most fascinating thing about the market was the sheer range of craft-work and antiques on offer: painted folk-puppets, silver jewellery, woven baskets – things hard to find in those places, like Thailand, that have been mobbed by souvenir-hungry visitors. Among the most memorable things about any place where the Burmese congregate are the women and girls, with their cheeks and foreheads smeared with what looks like pale yellow dust. This is a cosmetic made from ground thanaka bark, which protects the skin from the fierce sunlight, though it does turn pretty faces into quite alarming masks.

The evening in Pagan was entrancing. I'd been guided to the Aye Yeiktha Restaurant, which has a terrace overlooking the Shwezigon Pagoda that was lit up and shining white under a full moon – and, yes, the stars did twinkle. That would have been enough but, better still, the food was also good. There was a huge array of small dishes – pork fried with dried chilli, fried aubergine with chilli and shallots, the spicy split-pea fritters the old woman had been eating in the temple, curried this and curried that, and all around the supporting dishes of spicy vegetables. As well as the split-pea fritters, there were a number of other dishes with beans and lentils, which are normally little used in the other countries of the region and which are clearly another borrowing from India. What was very apparent was the taste of peanuts – growing nearby, and used both as an ingredient and as oil. If you wish to add a 'Pagan touch' to the recipes in this section, you could cook with the sort of distinctively flavoured nut oil usually intended for salad dressings, rather than the blander nut cooking oils.

Lacquerware is probably the country's major craft and, on the morning of my departure by car for Mandalay, a visit was organized to the U Ba Nyein Lacquer shop, which is also a school. There I was able to see the delicate hand-painting that produces the intricate traditional patterns, usually red-orange on a shiny black background, for bowls, trays and boxes. The people at the school had kindly laid on a breakfast of sweet coffee with black sticky rice, where the dark-coloured skin is cooked with the grains in coconut and palm sugar. There were also twice-fried beans and deep-fried batter sticks, a Chinese delicacy now eaten all over Asia, usually dipped in sticky-sweet condensed milk – a treat remembered from childhood.

After that, it was off for the long drive over hilly country to the northern capital, where the kings of Myanmar held court before the British arrived. It was a wonderful journey and my one chance to see something of the Burmese countryside, whenever we were able to stop for a rest.

The famous 'Road to Mandalay' of the poem and song is, of course, the river. The actual road doesn't follow the Irrawaddy at all, but heads off inland, starting on the flat river plain, rising into uplands before descending back to level ground as it begins its approach to the city. The journey takes almost a day, but offers a series of intriguing glimpses of Burmese life. We had no sooner left Pagan and were travelling through quite dense patches of forest when we came to a clearing where a large group of bullock carts, perhaps as many as a hundred, were gathered to collect water from a standpipe. Even one such cart is now a rare sight in many parts of Asia, so to stumble on an army of them seemed little short of miraculous. The light brown ridge-backed beasts, two to each cart, were dreamily patient, tails flicking away the flies, as their drivers manipulated them into neat lines to await their turn at the pump. The carts themselves were finely made, with an elegantly curved middle yoke and wavy halters and a fenced platform for the driver and his water container, high above the large wooden wheels. Bullocks are used to pull similarly designed ploughs that turn the rice paddies before the planting season, and many villages

have superb festival carts with sweeping side-rails and elaborately carved halters, with a carved figure balanced on a bar between the two yokes. After each cart had filled up its water tank the driver would urge his team away at a trot, whooping and yelling as they headed for home.

What this sight brought home to me was the main division within Burmese agriculture – the distinct difference between north and south, or Upper and Lower Burma, as they are usually called. Lower Burma, closer to the sea and the river deltas, has always had an easier time because of its abundant rainfall and natural irrigation. Rice is sown in June, transplanted to prevent overcrowding in September, reaped in December or January, and that is that. No manure is needed, beyond the ashes of the stubble which is burned every year. One crop a year is all that is required. In Upper Burma it is a different story. Poor rainfall means that rice must be cultivated in marked-off plots with carefully maintained irrigation ditches and some means of transferring water. When the shoots are about 30cm high and are moved from the nursery plots to the main paddies, they must have a bountiful and constant supply of water or they will yellow and droop.

Later that day we saw this process in action – a group of distant figures out in the flooded fields, men and women, knee-

Nats with placatory offerings

deep in water, bent double plucking up rice shoots for transplanting. While this was a sight you can see anywhere in the East, what made it different was a nearby water wheel, which was lifting water from one side of a restraining dike to the other. Like the carts, this was a carefully made affair of hand-carved spars, holding a wheel about 4m across, with bamboo spokes and a circle of blades. The wheel was operated by a man sitting on a high chair, legs pounding like mad, to keep up the flow. It was an irresistible sight, so it was off with the shoes and socks and into the squelchy mud for a sticky paddle over to the machine. As I could not communicate with the peddler or the planters it was only when I got back to the minibus that the driver was able to explain that this constant irrigation and transplanting were necessary near to Mandalay, where the farmers try to get up to three yearly rice harvests from their limited plots. As this could exhaust the land, they rotate their crops, changing from rice to millet and cotton or maize and beans. They also need some manure, and occasionally turn their buffaloes out on the paddies, which also churns up the land. They call this 'tickling the soil to make it laugh'. The driver didn't seem very fond of Burmese buffaloes, who were, he said, dirty and bad-tempered.

Of course, all these varieties of rice are confined to the relatively low-lying areas of the country. As elsewhere, the hill-tribes in the mountains lead a much more precarious existence, with slash-and-burn agriculture on small clearings, often with poor soil and unpredictable rainfall. This means that they must plant whatever will grow – rice if possible but, if it is too dry, then Indian corn, buckwheat or peas and beans. Although there is considerable variation in cooking among the different tribes, there is some similarity with the food of Northern Thailand and Laos, with the same emphasis on hunted meat and the gathering of wild vegetables and plants. There is also a similar production of charcuterie, such as Shan sausage, one of the few hill-tribe foods that you can find in Rangoon and other lowland cities.

What all the different regions share is a belief in spirits that the Burmese call Nats, and when we continued our journey and stopped for a break at a village we were invited to visit the hall that had been built to house these troublesome figures. You see, Nats are often mischievous, if not downright nasty, and have to be placated or else! Most Southeast Asians believe in spirits – in Thailand, Laos and Cambodia you often see spirit-houses put up as homes for the spirit of the land, lest he get mad because his domain has been usurped. In Burma, though, it goes much further

**Water-wheel beside the road
from Pagan to Mandalay**

**Cleaning a
bespectacled Buddha**

than that. I had already noticed shrines to individual Nats in Rangoon and Pagan, but seeing them all together – there are 37 main Nats – and seeing how important they clearly were to this small village, brought home that this was almost another religion, running parallel with Buddhism.

Some Nats are historical figures, others mythological characters. There are men and women Nats, and each covers a special area of human activity – love, business, health, etc. They are represented by brightly painted and gaudily dressed carved figures, holding the symbols of their power – a sword, some flowers, a silk scarf. Most Nats don't look nasty; many smile, some are quite comic, like figures from a children's story, but that is deceptive and you have to keep them happy with gifts of food and drink and money or they will get back at you.

I bought some bananas at the entrance and went into the long room where they were all lined up, and judiciously picked out any I thought looked a bit tricky, giving each some fruit or sticking a bank note in a hand or inside a costume. The trouble was, I didn't know which was which. I really wanted to get on the right side of the travel Nat in order to ward off any accidents, and I was rather hoping there might be a Nat in charge of food or restaurants; but all I could do was guess. I was told later that there is a Nat who helps out if you eat something bad. The appropriate prayer goes: 'Oh Lord, make the heat of my body go down, let my eating be good and my fever leave.' Which is worth remembering.

Outside, a large bus had drawn up and food sellers were clustered around the travellers, offering them trays of snacks. The Burmese are great eaters of little nibbles – they are on sale everywhere and people consume them all day long, though this doesn't seem to spoil their enthusiasm for the main meals of the day. I noticed the same split-pea fritters I'd seen in Pagan, along with a tray of 'little birds', tiny deep-fried birds that are crunched whole. There was also lots of fried chicken and plenty of fruit, great heaps of bright yellow jackfruit segments as well as baskets of the little sweet bananas. Hawking these snacks is good business for those local people lucky enough to live along the main bus routes. When we stopped at a tiny hamlet a few hours farther on, I saw a man working at a flat griddle, dry-frying brown flat bread, similar to Indian nan. This was clearly a full-time job, supplying the sellers who wait at the roadside. He was fun to watch, skil-

fully tossing his round 'pancakes' in the air so that they landed neatly on his hot-plate.

It was nearly nightfall as we approached Mandalay, but we made one last stop at a village that specializes in brewing palm wine. Tall palm trees surrounded a pretty cluster of dark wooden houses and I could see distant figures running up the thin trees – way, way up under the leaves – to drain away the liquid. This has to be quickly fermented and drunk the same day. The slightly foaming palm wine must be drunk before it turns into a very strong soup that will give a bad headache and an upset stomach the following day. Even fresh, it is very potent and, just off the road, I entered a compound where most of the village menfolk seemed to be lying around in palm wine dreamland, to judge by the absent grins on their faces.

I decided to walk farther on into the village, a place of handsome teakwood houses. The winding paths were lined with the toddy palms, and mango and jackfruit trees. There were more fruit trees around each compound's private vegetable plot, where I saw peas and beans growing, and plenty of large earthenware jars in which river fish would be fermenting, the principal source of flavouring. Indeed, watching the women prepare the evening meal while their husbands got merrily sozzled, I felt very much at home. If this was 'real' Burmese food, it was clearly part of that central Southeast Asian tradition that I had seen all through my travels – plenty of rice, curried catfish from the nearby stream and some

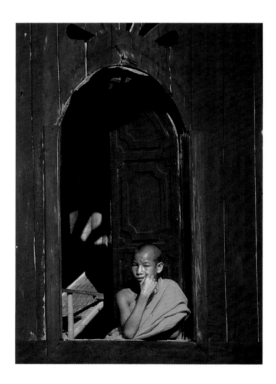

Novice monk near Lake Inle

highly spiced stir-fried watercress picked at the water's edge. The principal tastes are garlic and fermented or pickled fish, and there is plentiful use of turmeric – the main source of gingery flavour in Burmese food – which also gives many dishes their typical orange-yellow hue.

The village had a Nat shrine at its centre – just three Nats this time, all with reassuring smiles on their faces. Still, I gave them a bow and a bank note before we headed off on the last stage of what had proved an amazing journey.

There is no doubt that Mandalay, with its famous temples and its relics of Burma's royal past, is one of those dream destinations that every serious traveller hopes to see one day. Indeed it would have been the high spot of my visit if I hadn't already been to Pagan, after which nothing could ever compete. I seriously advise future visitors to the country to go first to Mandalay, then down to Pagan, which should be the very last place you visit in

Burma. Happily, the visit to Mandalay was redeemed by a spectacular event that was totally unexpected and all the better for it. I had gone to the Maha Muni Pagoda to see the huge, gold, seated statue of the Buddha, which is getting bigger by the minute, thanks to a constant stream of men who buy little sheets of gold leaf that they smear on to the enormous figure. They can put their gold wherever they wish, except on the face, and can climb up and walk behind it, to reach up to the top of the head. It is a strange and mysterious sight, to see the little gilded flakes shimmering on the vast body. No one knows exactly how much precious metal has been stuck to the Buddha over the years, but the effect is awesome. Oddly enough, among the few examples of modern technology I saw in use in Burma were the television cameras strategically arranged around the statue so that female worshippers, who may not climb up behind the statue, can still have an all-round view of proceedings on television sets placed about the temple.

It was as I was leaving the building that the great event happened. I suddenly found myself engulfed in a procession of fabulously clothed merrymakers, all in traditional costume. Groups of family and friends surrounded the doll-like figures of young boys dressed in white robes with coloured head-dresses, going into the local monastery to be novice monks during the rains. I had stumbled on a Shinpyu Ceremony, when boys aged seven and upwards become temporary monks at the beginning of the Buddhist New Year – their sisters get their ears pierced! It was a sumptuous spectacle, with those who could afford it paying for their sons to ride on richly caparisoned elephants. This was the India of the Maharajas – a reminder that Buddhism originally came from India and Sri Lanka, bringing so many other traditions with it, many of them Hindu in origin. The supporters wore coloured turbans and costumes embroidered with gold and beads, while the little novices were shaded by fringed silk parasols, the mahouts carefully directing their swaying beasts, as those below played instruments and clapped and shouted and danced alongside.

I wished I could follow them, aware that there would be a monster feast at some point in all the celebrations, and aware too that I would certainly have been invited to join in, because one always is. I was told later that rich families, like those who had hired the elephants, always offer at least four meat dishes and four fish and seafood, as well as vegetables, soup and rice. Middle-class families might get an Indian caterer to make a large meat and rice platter, while poorer families would just offer a rice and a curry dish with some pickles. I have to admit I would have followed an elephant if I could, but I had friends waiting at the Sa Khan Thar, which I had been told was Mandalay's best restaurant and where the owner Daw Kin Ma Lay was waiting to welcome me.

We ate outside under an enormous tamarind tree, its furry pods dangling down like Christmas decorations. Before the meal, Daw Kin Ma Lay took me into her kitchen, where a line of cooks was furiously at work, chopping and stir-frying. Daw Kin Ma Lay is one of the new breed of Burmese businesswomen who, like my friend in Rangoon, are trying to get the country ready to rejoin the

Nun reading a Buddhist text in Sagaing

world community. The Sa Khan Thar is one of the rare places where you can eat the sort of Burmese food normally found only in private houses, and that night we had a feast which ranged over the whole spectrum of flavours that encompasses Burma's Indian and Southeast Asian roots. There were fried sweetcorn cakes with crispy shallots at one end of the spectrum, crispy fried duck at the other, with hints of Thailand in a hot-and-sour fish cake salad. One of my friends went out to the street, where a travelling pickle-seller was offering mixtures of sweet-and-sour pickled fruits – mango, rose apple and a bitter fruit halfway between a plum and an olive – from large, wonderfully coloured glass jars, set up on a hand-drawn wagon.

As I feasted under the stars in Mandalay, it was clear to me that such food could be immensely popular outside Burma. I can see it finding great success in those countries like Britain that have already learned to love Indian and Chinese food – with Burmese food you get both, and more. For the moment it is virtually impossible to eat true Burmese food outside the country, except for the occasional restaurant in California. Of course, the first step is for the Burmese themselves to perfect the art of serving a domestic cuisine to a passing public, and with the likes of Daw Kin Ma Lay that is starting to happen. Next will be the moment when the world discovers Burma itself – and with Pagan on offer that is certainly going to happen. Until then, this unique food – like its country of origin – will have to remain one of the world's great secrets.

WET TAUK-TAUK GYAW

PORK FRIED WITH DRIED CHILLI

INGREDIENTS

- 2 tablespoons oil
- 2 garlic cloves, finely chopped
- 2 large dried red chillies, coarsely chopped
- 115g (4oz) pork, thinly sliced
- 60g (2oz) cauliflower, cut into small florets
- 60g (2oz) carrots, thinly sliced
- 1 tablespoon fish sauce
- 1 tablespoon light soy sauce
- ½ teaspoon sugar
- 2 spring onions, finely chopped

I ate this in Pagan, on the Aye Yeiktha Restaurant terrace with its spectacular view across to the illuminated Shwezigon Pagoda. This is a full dish for a main meal and should be served with a number of vegetable side-dishes, like the Bamboo Shoots Stir-fried with Spice Paste (page 149) and the Fried Sweetcorn with Crispy Shallots (see below).

PREPARATION

Heat the oil in a wok or deep frying pan and fry the garlic until golden. Add the chillies and stir briefly. Add the pork and stir-fry until almost cooked through.

Add all the remaining vegetables in succession, stirring once between each addition. Add the fish sauce, soy sauce and sugar, and stir briefly.

Remove from the heat and quickly stir in the spring onions. Turn out on a plate and serve.

PYAUNG-BU GYAW

FRIED SWEETCORN WITH CRISPY SHALLOTS

INGREDIENTS

- 3 cobs of fresh sweetcorn
- 2 tablespoons oil
- 6 small shallots, thinly sliced
- Salt and pepper

This was one of several delicious 'side dishes' served by Daw Kin Ma Lay at the Sa Khan Thar Restaurant in Mandalay. It goes especially well with Daw Kin Ma Lay's Crispy Duck (see page 154) and the Burmese Hot Sauce (see page 146).

PREPARATION

Using a large sharp knife and setting the cobs on their ends, remove the sweetcorn kernels from the uncooked cobs, Set aside.

Heat the oil in a frying pan which has a tight-fitting lid and fry the shallots until crispy. Remove, drain and set aside.

Reheat the oil, add the sweetcorn and stir. Cover the pan and cook until the corn softens, about 5 minutes.

Remove from the heat, add the crispy shallots and season to taste with salt and pepper. Turn out on a dish and serve.

NGA-PE THOKE
HOT-AND-SOUR FISH CAKE SALAD

INGREDIENTS
- I large dried red chilli, finely chopped
- I teaspoon finely chopped fresh turmeric
- I teaspoon finely chopped garlic
- I tablespoon finely chopped shallot
- ¼ teaspoon salt
- 450g (Ilb) white fish fillets (such as cod, monkfish, etc.), broken into flakes
- A mixture of assorted salad vegetables, such as shredded lettuce leaves, onion rings, cucumber slices, tomato wedges, chopped spring onions and coriander leaves, to serve

FOR THE DRESSING:
- 3 tablespoons fish sauce
- 3 tablespoons lime juice
- I tablespoon sugar
- 4 small fresh red or green chillies, finely chopped

PREPARATION
In a mortar, pound together the chilli, turmeric, garlic and shallot to make a paste. Add the salt, then add the flakes of fish and pound together. Using your fingers, divide the paste in two and mould both halves into a sausage shape.

Place in the upper compartment of a steamer and steam for 15-20 minutes, until solid.

While the fishcake is steaming, make the dressing: mix all the ingredients in a bowl.

When the fishcake is cooked, remove and cut into slices about 5mm (¼in) thick. Arrange the salad vegetables on a serving platter. Arrange the fish cake slices on top and either pour the dressing over the salad, tossing well, or serve it in a separate bowl for diners to use as they wish.

NGAN-BYA-YE DHYAW
BURMESE HOT SAUCE

INGREDIENTS
- I tablespoon oil
- I tablespoon finely chopped fresh turmeric
- I tablespoon dried shrimp, pounded to powder
- I teaspoon chilli powder
- 3 tablespoons fish sauce

PREPARATION
Heat the oil in a wok or deep frying pan and briefly fry the turmeric. Add the powdered shrimp and briefly stir-fry again.

Remove from the heat and add the chilli powder and fish sauce. Stir, turn into a dipping bowl and serve.

MON-LA-DOKE-THOKE
WHITE CABBAGE SALAD

INGREDIENTS
- 225g (8oz) white cabbage
- I onion, thinly sliced
- 2 small fresh red chillies, finely chopped
- ½ teaspoon salt
- I tablespoon lime juice
- I tablespoon peanut (groundnut) oil
- I tablespoon dried shrimp, pounded to powder

PREPARATION
Chop the white cabbage into thin rounds, then break these up with your fingers so that they fall apart into small twisted pieces. Place them in a bowl. Add the other ingredients and stir well.

NGAR-ASAT-KYAW
FRIED FISH WITH CRISPY CHILLI, GARLIC AND SHALLOTS

INGREDIENTS

- 1 teaspoon ground turmeric
- 1 whole medium-sized firm-fleshed fish, filleted and cut into 2.5cm (1in) pieces
- 2 tablespoons oil
- 4 small shallots, thinly sliced
- 2 garlic cloves, thinly sliced
- 2 large dried red chillies, coarsely chopped
- Oil for deep-frying
- 2 teaspoons salt
- ½ teaspoon sugar

PREPARATION

Use trout or sea bass for this dish Sprinkle the turmeric over the fish pieces and leave to marinate for 20 minutes. Meanwhile, heat the 2 tablespoons of oil in a wok or deep frying pan and fry the shallots until crispy. Remove, drain and set aside. Repeat the process with the garlic and the chillies. Reserve the oil. Heat the oil for deep-frying and fry the marinated fish until golden. Remove and drain. Reheat the reserved first oil in the wok or deep frying pan. Add the deep-fried fish and stir. Add the crispy shallots, garlic and chilli, and stir. Add the salt and sugar, and stir. Turn out on a plate and serve.

HKAYAN-THI PYOT-KYAW
FRIED AUBERGINE WITH CHILLI AND SHALLOTS

INGREDIENTS

- 4 small fresh red or green chillies
- 2 garlic cloves
- 4 small shallots
- 2 tablespoons oil
- 225g (8oz) aubergine, quartered lengthways, then cut into large cubes
- ½ teaspoon salt
- 1 teaspoon sugar
- 3 tablespoons vegetable stock (see page 14)

PREPARATION

In a mortar, pound the chillies, garlic and shallots to make a paste. In a frying pan which has a matching tight-fitting lid, heat the oil and stir in the paste. Add the aubergine and stir (well for green, less for black). Flavour with the salt and sugar, add the stock and stir. Cover and cook for up to 5 minutes, depending on which type of aubergine is being used. Turn out on a dish and serve.

THAKHWA-THI HIN-GYO
CUCUMBER AND DRIED SHRIMP SOUP

INGREDIENTS

- 2 tablespoons small dried shrimps
- 1 teaspoon shrimp paste (see page 14)
- 1 litre (1¾ pints) vegetable stock (see page 14)
- 2 tablespoons oil
- 1 garlic clove, finely chopped
- ½ teaspoon finely chopped fresh turmeric
- 225g (8oz) cucumber, peeled and finely diced
- 2 tablespoons fish sauce
- ½ teaspoon sugar
- ½ teaspoon pepper

PREPARATION

In a mortar, pound half the dried shrimps to a powder, reserving the other half. In a bowl, mix the shrimp paste with 2 tablespoons of the vegetable stock and set aside. In a large pan, heat the oil and fry the garlic and turmeric until the garlic is golden. Pour the remainder of the stock into the pan and mix. Add the cucumber, the reserved dried shrimps and the powdered dried shrimps, then stir in the shrimp paste and the remaining vegetable stock. Add the fish sauce, sugar and pepper. Bring to the boil and serve immediately.

WET-THA KHAUK-SWE-GYAW

STIR-FRIED NOODLES WITH PORK

INGREDIENTS

* 2 tablespoons oil
* 2 garlic cloves, finely chopped
* 1 teaspoon finely chopped ginger
* 1 large dried red chilli, coarsely chopped
* 225g (8oz) pork, thinly sliced
* 1 medium onion, finely chopped
* 1 tablespoon fish sauce
* 1 tablespoon light soy sauce
* 1 teaspoon sugar
* 225g (8oz) medium flat white flour noodles, soaked and drained (see page 11)
* 115g (4oz) celery, coarsely chopped

There is a large, two-storey dragon boat permanently moored in the moat that surrounds the remains of the Royal Palace in Mandalay. Used as a restaurant, it is more of a curiosity than a gourmet's paradise, but this variation of a classic Asian noodle dish was a happy choice for me when I visited the establishment.

PREPARATION

Heat the oil in a wok or deep frying pan and fry the garlic until golden.

Add the ginger and stir. Add the chilli and stir. Then add the pork and stir well until it is just cooked through.

Add the onion and stir. Add the fish sauce, soy sauce and sugar, and stir once. Then add the noodles and stir well for 1 minute.

Add the celery, stir briefly, turn out on a plate and serve.

BAYAGYAW

SPICY SPLIT-PEA FRITTERS

INGREDIENTS

* 115g (4oz) dried yellow split-peas, soaked overnight
* 1 medium onion, finely chopped
* 2 small fresh red chillies, finely chopped
* 2 kaffir lime leaves, finely chopped
* 1 tablespoon finely chopped coriander (leaf and stem)
* ½ teaspoon ground turmeric
* ½ teaspoon salt
* 1 tablespoon cornflour
* Oil for deep-frying

This dish can be used as a starter, though it is often served with drinks and may even appear with afternoon tea or coffee. It was the 'snack' the old lady had brought to the temple in Pagan, but it can be one of the 'side dishes' served with a curry.

PREPARATION

Drain the split-peas and place them in a bowl with 4 tablespoons water and all the other ingredients except the oil. Mix thoroughly to form a paste.

Heat the oil for deep-frying. Scoop up a heap of paste in one teaspoon and use a second to ease it into the hot oil. Repeat until all the paste has been used and all the oval pellets have been fried until golden brown, cooking in batches if necessary. Remove and drain the fritters as they are cooked, and serve immediately.

SEIK-THA HIN
LAMB WITH MINT LEAVES

INGREDIENTS

- 450g (1lb) lamb steaks, cubed
- ¼ teaspoon salt
- 1 teaspoon ground turmeric
- 2 tablespoons oil
- 2 garlic cloves, finely chopped
- ½ teaspoon ground cumin
- 1 medium onion, coarsely chopped
- 2 medium tomatoes, coarsely chopped
- 2 tablespoons fish sauce
- ½ teaspoon sugar
- 2 medium fresh red chillies, coarsely chopped
- 20 fresh mint leaves

PREPARATION

Place the lamb, salt and turmeric in a large pan with 225ml (8fl oz) water and bring to the boil. Cover and simmer for 1 hour.

Heat the oil in a wok or deep frying pan and fry the garlic until golden. Stir in the cumin.

Remove the meat from the water, drain well and add to the frying pan. Stir well, then add the onion, tomatoes, fish sauce, sugar and chillies, continuing to stir.

Remove from the heat, quickly stir in the mint leaves and serve.

PE-GYAN-GYAW
TWICE-COOKED SPLIT-PEAS

INGREDIENTS

- 175g (6oz) dried yellow split-peas, soaked overnight
- 2 tablespoons oil
- 2 garlic cloves, finely chopped
- 1 tablespoon finely chopped ginger
- 1 medium onion, coarsely chopped
- Salt to taste

PREPARATION

Remove the split-peas from their soaking water, transfer to a pan of fresh boiling water and simmer for 5 minutes. Remove, drain and set aside.

Heat the oil in a wok or deep frying pan and fry the garlic until golden. Add the ginger and briefly stir-fry. Add the onion and briefly stir-fry.

Add the split-peas and a sprinkling of salt to taste. Stir-fry for 2 minutes, then turn out on a plate and serve.

BE-GIN
CRISPY DUCK

INGREDIENTS

- 1 whole duck, about 1.85kg (4lb)
- 2 tablespoons five-spice powder
- 1 teaspoon salt
- ½ teaspoon pepper
- 1 teaspoon sugar
- Oil for deep-frying

PREPARATION

Evenly coat the duck inside and out with five-spice powder, salt, pepper and sugar. Place in the upper compartment of a steamer and steam for 15 minutes. Remove and let any water drain away.

With a Chinese axe or chopper, halve the duck lengthways and chop away the wings and legs. Then chop each half into small portions, roughly 2.5cm (1in) wide. Heat the oil and deep-fry the duck pieces until crispy. Remove them as they are cooked, drain well and serve.

AMETHA HIN

BEEF IN TAMARIND SAUCE

INGREDIENTS

- 2 medium dried red chillies, finely chopped
- 1 teaspoon finely chopped ginger
- 2 garlic cloves, finely chopped
- 6 small shallots, finely chopped
- 2 tablespoons oil
- 450g (1lb) beef, cubed
- 1 teaspoon ground turmeric
- 2 tablespoons fish sauce
- 2 tablespoons tamarind water (see page 19)

PREPARATION

In a mortar, pound together the chillies, ginger, garlic and shallots to form a paste.

Heat the oil and stir in the paste. Add the beef and stir well. Add the turmeric and fish sauce, and stir well. Add 350ml (12fl oz) water and bring back to the boil. Cover and simmer for 1 hour.

Finally, add the tamarind water, stir and simmer for a further 5 minutes. Turn out into a bowl and serve.

KYET-THA KHAUK-SWE-BYOKE

BURMESE CHICKEN NOODLE

INGREDIENTS

- 2 tablespoons oil
- 225ml (8fl oz) coconut milk
- 275g (10oz) chicken, thinly sliced
- 450ml (¾ pint) chicken stock (see page 14)
- 225g (8oz) egg noodles (see page 11)
- 2 tablespoons fish sauce
- 1 teaspoon sugar
- 1 tablespoon lemon juice

FOR THE CURRY PASTE:

- ½ teaspoon coriander seeds
- 1 teaspoon finely chopped fresh turmeric
- 1 teaspoon finely chopped ginger
- 1 large dried red chilli, finely chopped
- 3 small red shallots, finely chopped
- ¼ teaspoon salt

This is the classic Burmese noodle dish, one of the rare Burmese recipes known outside the country. It brings together perfectly many of the different influences that are part of Burmese cuisine. As I learned on my visit, there are considerable variations in how this national noodle dish is served. At the River View Restaurant in Pagan it was an elaborate affair in which most of the ingredients were served separately and mixed by the diners. This is the simple 'all-in-one' version I ate in Rangoon's Bogyoke Aung San Market.

You will need only 1 tablespoon of the curry paste for this dish; the rest will keep for several days in the refrigerator and can be used for many other dishes.

PREPARATION

First make the curry paste: in a mortar, pound the coriander seeds to a powder. Then add each ingredient in turn, pounding together to make a paste. Stir in the salt and set aside.

Heat the oil in a wok or deep frying pan and stir in 1 tablespoon of the curry paste. Add the coconut milk and stir well. Add the chicken and cook, stirring, until the meat is just cooked through.

Pour in the stock and bring back to the boil. Add the noodles and stir well. Add the fish sauce and sugar and stir well.

Remove from the heat and add the lemon juice. Stir once, pour into a bowl and serve.

KYAUK-KYAW

JELLY CUSTARD

INGREDIENTS
- 115g (4oz) agar agar jelly powder (see page 19)
- 225g (8oz) sugar
- 450ml (¾ pint) coconut milk
- 1 egg

This is a basic recipe that you can vary at will – the agar jelly is tasteless, so you can add sweet or savoury flavours to it. I've used coconut here, but I've come across flavours as varied as the juice squeezed from banyan leaves to instant coffee! More conventionally, you could replace the coconut milk with orange juice – or other fruit juices – and you could put a little chopped fruit into the moulds before pouring in the jelly.

PREPARATION
Put the agar agar jelly powder into a saucepan with 450ml (¾ pint) water and bring to the boil, stirring constantly.

Add the sugar and stir well. Add the coconut milk and stir as you bring back to the boil. Beat the egg and stir into the mixture. Simmer for a moment, then pour into moulds. Leave to set and cool.

Turn out (a quick dip in hot water will help) and serve.

MON-LET-SAUNG

SAGO WITH PALM SUGAR AND COCONUT MILK

INGREDIENTS
- 225ml (8fl oz) dried sago
- 450ml (¾ pint) coconut milk
- 225g (8oz) palm sugar (see page 19)

PREPARATION
Wash the sago in cold water and drain.

In a pan, heat 450ml (¾ pint) fresh water. Add the sago and bring to the boil. When the sago floats to the surface, it is cooked. Remove with a slotted spoon as it rises and place in a bowl of cold water.

When all the sago is transferred, remove from the cold water and drain. Place in a serving bowl and set aside.

In a saucepan, heat the coconut milk. Add the palm sugar and stir until dissolved, then transfer to another serving bowl.

Serve the sago and this warm sauce separately, allowing diners to mix them as they wish. In summer the sago can be served cold with crushed ice.

Malaysia an

Singapore

TOMORROW TODAY

When the railway line running south from Bangkok was finally completed, early in the 20th century, it brought to an end centuries of division and conflict by linking Thailand to its southern neighbour, the then British colony of Malaya. At the time, it was a miracle of engineering, running from the banks of the Chao Phya River, across the narrow isthmus of southern Thailand to the Andaman Sea, through dense jungle and water-logged rice paddies, on across the border, skirting the Cameron Highlands to Kuala Lumpur, for the final leg over the Straits of Jahore to Singapore Island.

Poultry seller, Central Market, Kota Bharu, Malaysia

It was no easy ride and even today the journey still takes three days and nights, with travellers needing to bring their own supplies to augment the limited meals available on board. The coming of aircraft made this seem even more arduous, reducing the train's customers to the very poor, the occasional backpacker from Europe and the few who were just passionate about railways and who could still see the charm of the Victorian fretwork stations dotted along the line, as if little fantasy English villages had been set down right in the middle of Asia.

All that changed in 1993 when the company that runs the Orient Express, the luxury train that travels between London and Venice, decided to put something similar, the Eastern and Oriental Express, on the old Thailand-Malaysia line. Carriages were fitted with rosewood and mahogany cabins and suites, with lamps by Lalique and Baccarat crystal for the dining rooms and bars. There were leather armchairs for the library and the train was staffed with chefs, waiters, traditional dancers and even a fortune-teller, to help the 36 hours from Bangkok to Singapore pass without a dull moment.

Despite its drawbacks, I was one of the few who loved the old train. I used to travel from Bangkok's Hua Lampong Station, with its high arches and Italianate tile floors, on the four-hour journey to the tiny gingerbread station at Hua Hin on the eastern coast, the prettiest of all the stations because it served the King's seaside villa. Even I have to admit, however, that the luxuries of having breakfast in bed off a silver tray in my own cabin aboard the new train, or drinking cocktails on the open observation deck at nightfall, take some beating.

The food on board is supervised by head chef Kevin Cape, who is based in Bangkok where he is able to stock up with fresh ingredients just before the train leaves. If there is anything special on offer at any of the stations, he can buy more en route. The meals served are a mix of Eastern and Western ideas, the sort of blend that in recent years has enlivened the cooking of many young chefs in London, New York and California. Today, there are few leading cooks who don't find some use for lemon grass and chillies, and I've included in this chapter a beancurd soup from the train's menu that shows how delicious this sort of inventiveness can be. There is nothing inauthentic about this type of cooking — indeed the region of southern Thailand that the train crosses is famous for its blend of Thai and Malaysian cooking styles.

Malaysian food, like the country and its people, is an intricate web of world-wide influences born of its strategic position astride the main sea route linking Europe, Arabia, India, China and the Far East. It was the Port of Malacca (present day Melaka) on the western coast of the peninsula that drew spice traders from Europe, following where the Indians had led. Indian traders were visiting the peninsula early in the Christian era and by the end of the 13th century AD Muslim voyagers from the sub-continent had brought Islam, the dominant religion of modern Malaysia.

Two centuries later, Malacca had fallen to the Portuguese and by 1641 to the Dutch. They were finally out-manoeuvred at the end of the 18th century when the British set up a rival port on the island of Penang, which quickly replaced Malacca as the main centre of the Southeast Asian trade route. Initially the British were interested only in these coastal trading ports, establishing another settlement at Singapore. Gradually, however, the inland sultanates were drawn into agreements and unions, and by the early years of the 20th century the entire peninsula was effectively transformed into a colony. This in turn, drew tens of thousands of

Chinese immigrants as coolie labour, and others came later as traders, until they were almost as numerous as the original Malays.

Only an outside power could have held this volatile mix together, but the humiliating defeat by the invading Japanese in 1942 shattered the illusion of British invincibility. When the war ended and colonial rule was re-established, it was only a question of time before independence would come, though there was still a protracted jungle war against communist insurgents and a great deal of manoeuvring to satisfy the claims and fears of the different communities before the present state of harmony was achieved.

Today there are two separate nations: Malaysia and Singapore. Malaysia consists of the original peninsula, now joined by the two states that occupy the northern rim of the island of Borneo across the South China Sea — Sabah and Sarawak, once ruled by the descendants of the British adventurer James Brooke, the 'White Raja'. The second state, wealthy and successful far beyond its tiny dimensions, is the island-city of Singapore. Its predominantly Chinese population made continuing relations with the increasingly Malay-dominated state to the north difficult — with it eventually separating from the union in 1965.

Whatever their political differences, Malaysia and Singapore have much in common. Both have such a variety of cultures and religions that they celebrate New Year four times a year and both share a range of culinary influences that is almost a history of world food. In the simplest terms, true Malaysian cooking is rich and aromatic, heavily spiced but lightened with herb flavours, tamarind sourness and fish saltiness taken from its northern neighbours. This mix is easiest seen in the ubiquitous satay, a dish that clearly echoes the Arabic kebab, though its accompanying peanut sauce merges Indian spices with Southeast Asian herb and fish flavours. In the main centres, especially independent Singapore, later waves of Indian and Chinese immigrants have remained loyal to the culinary traditions of their places of origin, so that the visitor is offered a wide choice — from Malay cooking to Cantonese and Kashmiri cuisine, or even an English steak and kidney pudding if you so desire.

Of course, most first-time visitors to Malaysia see only the main sites of the Western Peninsula, where the population is divided 60/30 between ethnic Malays and Malay-Chinese, with the remaining 10 per cent of Indian origin. It is the food of the two largest groups that most interests me, especially when they come together. Many Chinese arrived in the region in the late 18th and early 19th centuries, subsequently settling and marrying Malay or Indonesian wives. These 'Straits' or 'Baba' Chinese lived in two worlds, their descendants — the 'Peranakan' or 'children of mixed race' — even more so. Their homes looked Chinese and they wore Chinese clothes, but the food they ate was nonya, the word for their mother, who followed her own Malay culinary traditions with a leavening of Chinese recipes introduced to please her husband.

Bullock cart, Malaysia

Nonya food is one of the great cuisines of Asia, but is hard to find outside Peranakan homes. Even there it is thought to be dying out, as the modern descendants of the settlers have started to veer either to their Chinese or to their Malay ancestry, abandoning the middle ground. Nonya cooking has two main centres – Singapore, of course, but also Penang, the tiny island off the north-west coast of the peninsula, where the Eastern and Oriental Express makes its first long stop on the journey south.

As the train pulled into Butterworth Station on the mainland we were greeted by drums, bells and a Chinese lion weaving its dance of welcome. Penang is a 15-minute ferry ride across the narrow straits to Georgetown, which, as its name suggests, was a British creation – now largely inhabited by Chinese, or rather their Peranakan descendants, whose culture dominates the island. Acquired by Captain Francis Light in 1786 as a trading post for the East India Company, it was named for the future King George IV. The tiny town was established during one of the best periods in British architecture, which has left the gracious sea-front centre around Fort Cornwallis fringed with elegant white Regency and Georgian porticoes.

This was the setting for the brief tour that the train passengers were able to make. As I had already visited the island some years earlier, I could also recall the Chinese quarter, with its fabulous carved and coloured temples and Clan Houses, heavy with incense, and the line of somewhat shabby but still imposing Chinese merchants' mansions along Millionaire's Row, on the way to the best beaches and the new tourist hotels. My happiest memories were of animals in public places: the snakes, some of them poisonous, roaming more or less freely round the bluntly named Snake Temple, and the tribes of mischievous macaque monkeys fighting for control of territory in the Botanic Gardens.

Georgetown itself has a little museum in what was once a British school and when I visited it in the late eighties it had an appealingly faded air. There were few other visitors to share my fascination with the collection of photographs and souvenirs of turn-of-the-century Penang. At the rear of the building were room settings and costumes that showed something of Peranakan life – the Baba and Nonya in their long embroidered Chinese wedding robes, and the sort of inlaid lacquered furniture that I then thought unique. Since my visit to Hoi An in Vietnam, however, I now know this to be part of a shared culture that these intrepid Chinese travellers spread all round the South China Sea, in the trading ports where they settled, leading a new life while still haunted by the old one that they had left behind.

The food they created could still be enjoyed on Gurney Drive after nightfall, where restaurants and food stalls offered everything from 'pure' Indian, Chinese and Malay dishes to the nonya versions that drew on all these traditions to create something unique. There is a distinct difference between the two centres of nonya

The statue of Singapore's founder, Sir Stamford Raffles, surrounded by the towering symbols of the city's success

cooking: in Singapore the use of creamy coconut milk sauces and a slightly heavier hand with dry spices shows the influence of southern Malay and Indonesian traditions; by contrast Penang has more of the sour lemon/lime tastes of neighbouring Thailand, and sauces are lighter and more liquid. Both these traditions merge in Laksa Lemak, the noodle dish strongly flavoured with coconut milk (see page 170), that veers towards India with hints of tamarind and turmeric, then back East with fish sauce and shrimp paste. Penang and Singapore have their own versions of the dish and in Penang you should try Penang laksa, with fish.

Sadly, there was no time to repeat that treat, though we did take a brief rickshaw ride around the town before going back on board the train for afternoon tea. This very English custom still lives on in Malaysia. The railway line skirts the Cameron Highlands and the tea plantations where the British settled, and where their friends used to come for a break from the tropical heat of Kuala Lumpur. In the midst of dense jungle inhabited by tribal peoples who, if the warning signs by the side of the highway are to be believed, still capture and kill anyone foolish enough to stray from the main roads, the British built a dream world of mock-Tudor hotels. Some years ago, I stayed at Ye Olde Smokehouse with its log fires, horse brasses and inglenooks, where I found Devon cream teas with scones and strawberry jam. Today, Malaysian families still drive up for tea and have themselves photographed in front of these eccentric reminders of a way of life that now seems barely credible.

The same is true of Kuala Lumpur railway station, where the train made a brief midnight stopover, just long enough to see the British imagination at its most fantastical. This time the architecture is an astonishing mix of Arabic, Gothic and Greek. It is a fitting prelude to the city itself, for 'KL', as everybody calls it, is built around a cricket pitch, the pedang, with a mock-Tudor clubhouse. There, men in whites bowl and bat and ignore the fact that enormous skyscrapers – mighty symbols of the rocketing success of this 'tiger' economy – now loom over their village green. Even religion has been caught up in the drive for growth. One of the city's finest modern creations is the Masjid Negara, the National Mosque, a vast construction that can accommodate hundreds of worshippers at Friday prayers. A mountain of shoes piles up at the entrances, as the men in their sarongs and songkok caps face Mecca in unison, the air cooled by shimmering pools of water whose reflections play on the marble walls and tiled floors.

Like the other capitals of the free-wheeling Asian economies, KL has enjoyed almost unbelievable growth, though it has been lucky to have a solid infrastructure laid out in the colonial era. As in Rangoon, there are gardens and parks and flower beds, good basic sanitation and a manageable road system. Far from being oppressive, squalid and polluted, the city still feels cool and relatively open.

So where do you eat in KL? In a revolving restaurant at the top of a tower? In the cavernous dining room of an international hotel? No, you go to a car park! Every night when the vehicles and buses have gone, an army of hawkers appears with little metal tables and

CILI KETMA
CHILLI CRAB

INGREDIENTS
- 4 fresh medium crabs
- 1 tablespoon finely chopped ginger
- 3 garlic cloves, finely chopped
- 4 fresh red or green chillies, finely chopped
- 1 teaspoon shrimp paste (see page 14)
- 4 tablespoons oil
- 2 tablespoons tomato purée
- 1 tablespoon fish sauce
- 1 tablespoon light soy sauce
- 1 teaspoon sugar

This is the one dish all Singaporeans insist you must eat, preferably at a seaside restaurant. It isn't as fearsomely hot as its name suggests – chilli is balanced by the sweetness of the tomato purée and sugar.

PREPARATION
If you buy live crabs, put the point of a knife into the shell between the eyes and strike the end of the handle a quick, hard blow – this kills the crab instantly and humanely. Cut away the undershell and discard the abdominal sac just behind the mouth. Break off the two large pincers and crack them open. With a Chinese chopper, quarter each crab. Set aside.

In a mortar, pound together the ginger, garlic and chillies to make a paste. Stir in the shrimp paste. Heat the oil in a wok or deep frying pan and fry the paste. Stir in the tomato purée and 2 tablespoons water. Add the crab pieces and stir well. Add the fish sauce, soy sauce and sugar and stir well, ensuring that the pieces are well coated. Turn out on a platter and serve.

KERANG TUMIS DENGAN CILI
MUSSELS WITH ONION, GARLIC AND CHILLI

INGREDIENTS
- 2 tablespoons oil
- 2 garlic cloves, finely chopped
- 4 small red shallots, thinly sliced
- 1 tablespoon finely chopped ginger
- 3 medium fresh red chillies, finely chopped
- 1 tablespoon yellow bean sauce (see page 14)
- 450g (1lb) mussels

Mussels should always be cleaned in several changes of water, with any that float being discarded. The principle is that those that are open before cooking must be thrown away, as should any that aren't open after cooking. Leave them overnight in a bucket of water with a good shake of porridge oats for them to feed on, they will eat and void themselves. Before cooking, you pull away the tiny beard and give the shells a good scrub to remove any barnacles.

PREPARATION
Heat the oil in a heavy-based pan which has a tight-fitting lid. Fry the garlic until golden. Add the shallots, ginger, chillies and bean sauce, and stir briefly.

Lift the mussels out of their last cleaning water and put them in the pan – any water that transfers with them should be enough for cooking purposes, but add a little more if you think the pan is too dry. Give the mussels one good stir. Cover the pan, turn up the heat and let them cook briefly – no more than 3 minutes, shaking the pan from time to time to ensure they cook evenly. Lift the lid to check all are open and discard any that are not.

Ensure each mussel gets a little of the sauce, then turn into bowls and serve.

SAMBAL KAEHAND PANJANG
PRAWN AND LONGBEAN SAMBAL

INGREDIENTS

- 2 large dried red chillies, finely chopped
- 8 small red shallots, finely chopped
- ½ teaspoon shrimp paste (see page 14)
- 2 tablespoons oil
- 2 tablespoons crushed peanuts
- 225g (8oz) raw prawns, peeled and deveined
- 225g (8oz) longbeans
- 125ml (4fl oz) coconut milk
- ½ teaspoon salt
- 1 teaspoon sugar

PREPARATION

In a mortar, pound together the chillies and shallots. Add the shrimp paste and mix well.

Heat the oil in a wok or deep frying pan and fry the paste. Add the peanuts and prawns. Stir well, then add the longbeans cut into 2.5cm (1in) lengths, coconut milk, salt and sugar.

Stir well for a few seconds, then turn into a bowl and serve.

SAMBAL IKAN
FISH SAMBAL

INGREDIENTS

- 2 small whole fish with rich 'meaty' flesh (such as mackerel)
- Oil for deep-frying
- 4 garlic cloves, finely chopped
- 8 small red shallots, coarsely chopped
- 1 stalk of lemon grass, finely chopped
- 3 large dried red chillies, finely chopped
- ½ teaspoon shrimp paste (see page 14)
- 2 teaspoons tamarind water (see page 19)
- 1 tablespoon sugar
- 1 tablespoon fish sauce

PREPARATION

Clean the fish and place in a deep pan. Add enough oil to come halfway up the fish, heat and fry the fish until it is golden brown, turning once. Remove, drain and place on a serving dish. Keep warm.

In a mortar, pound together the garlic, shallots, lemon grass and chillies to form a paste. Stir in the shrimp paste.

Put 2 tablespoons of the oil from the deep-frying into another frying pan, heat and stir in the paste. Add the tamarind water, 2 teaspoons water, the sugar and fish sauce.

Stir well, pour over the fried fish and serve.

FOO YONG HAI
CRAB MEAT AND BAMBOO SHOOT OMELETTE

INGREDIENTS

- 4 eggs
- 115g (4oz) cooked crab meat
- 115g (4oz) bamboo shoots, finely chopped
- 2 spring onions, finely chopped
- 1 tablespoon fish sauce
- ½ teaspoon sugar
- ¼ teaspoon black pepper
- 2 tablespoons oil

PREPARATION

In a bowl, beat the eggs and stir in all the ingredients except the oil.

Heat the oil in a frying pan and, when it is very hot, pour in the mixture. Leave to cook until the base of the omelette is firm and golden brown. Turn the omelette over and cook the other side in the same way.

Slide the omelette out on to a plate and serve.

SATAY AYAM
CHICKEN SATAY

INGREDIENTS

- 450g (1lb) chicken breast, preferably from a free-range or corn-fed bird
- 2 teaspoons coriander seeds
- ½ teaspoon cumin seeds
- 2 garlic cloves, coarsely chopped
- 1 teaspoon finely chopped ginger
- 1 teaspoon finely chopped fresh turmeric
- 4 small red shallots, finely chopped
- 1 teaspoon salt
- 2 tablespoons sugar
- 2 tablespoons oil
- 20 bamboo satay sticks, or equivalent

FOR THE SAUCE:

- 2 large dried red chillies, finely chopped
- 2 garlic cloves, finely chopped
- 1 stalk of lemon grass, finely chopped
- 1 teaspoon finely chopped fresh turmeric
- 2 tablespoons oil
- 450ml (¾ pint) coconut milk
- 1 tablespoon tamarind water (see page 19)
- 2 tablespoons sugar
- ½ teaspoon salt
- 4 tablespoons crushed peanuts

PREPARATION

If necessary, skin the chicken breasts and cut the meat away from the bone, then slice the meat into long thin strips, about 10×1cm (4×½in). Set aside.

In a mortar, pound together the coriander and cumin seeds, garlic, ginger, turmeric and shallots to make a paste. Stir in the salt, sugar and oil. Turn the mixture into a bowl, add the chicken strips and stir to coat thoroughly. Leave to marinate for 1 hour.

While the chicken is marinating, make the sauce: in a mortar, pound together the chilli, garlic, lemon grass and turmeric to form a paste.

Heat the oil in a wok or deep frying pan and stir in the paste. Add the coconut milk, stir well and bring to the boil. Add all the remaining ingredients in succession, stirring between each addition. Simmer for 3 minutes, then turn into a bowl.

When the chicken is marinated, fold each strip of chicken in a ripple and pierce this with a satay stick, through the folds as if sewing. Place the sticks under a hot grill or on a barbecue and turn from time to time, until cooked through. Serve with the sauce.

EGG SAMBAL
EGGS IN SPICY TOMATO SAUCE

INGREDIENTS

- 2 large dried red chillies, coarsely chopped
- 1 teaspoon finely chopped ginger
- 3 garlic cloves, finely chopped
- 8 small red shallots, finely chopped
- 3 tablespoons oil
- 5 tablespoons tomato purée
- 6 hard-boiled eggs, shelled
- 8 tablespoons coconut milk
- 2 teaspoons lemon juice
- 2 tablespoons sugar
- 1 teaspoon salt

A sambal is a very spicy side dish meant to add zest to other food. There should be at least one sambal with a well-balanced Malaysian meal.

PREPARATION

In a mortar, pound together the chillies, ginger, garlic and shallots to form a paste. Heat the oil in a wok or deep frying pan and stir in the paste. Add the tomato purée and stir well. Add the whole hard-boiled eggs and stir, coating well. Pour in the coconut milk and stir well. Add all the remaining ingredients, stir and simmer for 5 minutes. Turn into a bowl and serve.

SUP TAUHU
BEANCURD SOUP

INGREDIENTS

- 450ml (¾ pint) vegetable stock (see page 14)
- 115g (4oz) white beancurd, diced into 1cm (½in)cubes
- 30g (1oz) carrots, finely diced
- 30g (1oz) onion, finely diced
- 1 spring onion, thinly sliced
- 2 tablespoons light soy sauce
- 1 teaspoon sugar
- A sprinkling of freshly ground black pepper

This is my version of the soup served on the Eastern and Oriental Express. It is very mild and could be served, in the Asian way, not as a separate course but as part of a main course, a useful foil to a hot curry.

PREPARATION
Heat the stock, add the beancurd and bring to the boil. Stir in all the other ingredients except the pepper and serve.

MEE HOON GORENG
SINGAPORE FRIED NOODLES

INGREDIENTS

- 2 tablespoons oil
- 1 garlic clove, finely chopped
- 1 teaspoon curry powder (see page 15)
- 60g (2oz) small fresh shrimps
- 60g (2oz) barbecued pork (see page 183), cut into small cubes
- 1 egg, lightly beaten
- 225g (8oz) rice vermicelli (see page 11)
- 60g (2oz) beansprouts
- 60g (2oz) carrots, cut into thin matchsticks
- 1 tablespoon fish sauce
- 1 tablespoon light soy sauce
- 1 teaspoon sugar
- A sprinkling of black pepper

PREPARATION
Heat the oil in a wok or deep frying pan and fry the garlic until it is golden. Add the remaining ingredients in succession, stirring well between each addition.

As soon as the pepper is stirred in, turn out on a plate and serve.

GADO GADO

VEGETABLE SALAD WITH PEANUT SAUCE

INGREDIENTS

- Oil for deep-frying
- 2 blocks of beancurd, about 5cm (2in) square
- 115g (4oz) beansprouts
- 115g (4oz) longbeans, chopped into 2.5cm (1in) lengths
- 115g (4oz) cucumber, thinly sliced
- 115g (4oz) white cabbage, thinly sliced then broken up into strands
- 2 hard-boiled eggs

FOR THE PEANUT SAUCE:

- 2 large dried red chillies, finely chopped
- 2 garlic cloves, finely chopped
- 5 small red shallots, finely chopped
- ½ teaspoon shrimp paste (see page 14)
- 2 tablespoons oil
- 450ml (¾ pint) coconut milk
- ½ teaspoon salt
- 1 tablespoon sugar
- 1 teaspoon tamarind water (see page 19)
- 4 tablespoons crushed peanuts

PREPARATION

First make the sauce: in a mortar, pound together the chillies, garlic and shallots to form a paste. Add the shrimp paste and mix well.

Heat the oil in a wok or deep frying pan and stir in the paste. Add the coconut milk and stir well. Add all the remaining ingredients together, stirring well. Cook briefly until the coconut milk comes to the boil. Remove at once from the heat.

Make the salad: heat the oil and deep-fry the beancurd until golden. Remove, drain and set aside.

Arrange all the vegetables in a salad bowl. Shell the eggs and quarter them, then place in the salad bowl. Thinly slice the beancurd and place the slices in the bowl.

Serve with the sauce, either separately or poured over the salad and tossed.

OPOR AYAM

CHICKEN IN COCONUT

INGREDIENTS

- 1 medium chicken, about 1.25kg (2¾lb)
- 1 teaspoon coriander seeds
- ½ teaspoon cumin seeds
- 2 large dried red chillies, coarsely chopped
- 1 tablespoon finely chopped galangal
- 3 garlic cloves, finely chopped
- 1 teaspoon finely chopped ginger
- 1 teaspoon finely chopped fresh turmeric
- 8 small red shallots, finely chopped
- 3 tablespoons oil
- 1 stalk of lemon grass, chopped into 2.5cm (1in) lengths and slightly crushed
- 700ml (1¼ pints) coconut milk
- 4 kaffir lime leaves, coarsely chopped
- 2 teaspoons salt
- 1 tablespoon sugar

PREPARATION

Prepare the chicken: chop off the wings and legs, cut the carcass in half lengthways, then quarter it across; chop each quarter into 4 (you should now have 20 pieces of chicken). Set aside.

In a mortar, pound the coriander seeds, then add the cumin seeds and pound together. Add the chillies, galangal, garlic, ginger, turmeric and shallots and pound to form a paste.

Heat the oil in a large heavy-based pan and stir in the paste. Add the lemon grass and stir. Add 4 tablespoons of the coconut milk and stir. Add the chicken pieces and stir well. Add a further 6 tablespoons of the coconut milk and continue stirring. Add the kaffir lime leaves, salt and sugar, and stir. Add the remaining coconut milk and simmer for 30 minutes.

Turn into a bowl and serve.

PULOT HITAM
BLACK STICKY RICE PUDDING

INGREDIENTS
- 225g (8oz) black sticky rice (see page 11)
- 115g (4oz) white sticky rice
- 85g (3oz) sugar

TO SERVE:
- 225ml (8fl oz) coconut cream
- A pinch of salt

This is called black sticky rice pudding because the colour that predominates comes from the dark husk on the unpolished grains. Because these are too hard to use on their own, however, they have to be mixed with the much softer white grains. Nevertheless, it makes that very rare thing, a healthy pudding, as the husk is the most nutritious part of the grain.

Although I ate this in a restaurant in Singapore, it is eaten in homes all over Southeast Asia, and much loved by children because of its mix of sugary rice with slightly salty cream.

PREPARATION
Soak both types of sticky rice overnight, or for at least 6 hours.

Wash and drain them, then place them in a pan with 1.5 litres (2¾ pints) water and bring to the boil. Simmer, stirring from time to time, until the grains have absorbed all the water but are not yet dry. Add the sugar and stir well.

Turn into bowls and pour over a little coconut cream mixed with salt.

KUEH PISANG
BANANA PUDDING

INGREDIENTS
- 1 large banana
- 400ml (14fl oz) coconut cream
- 1 teaspoon rice flour
- 3 tablespoons sugar
- A pinch of salt

This is another pudding from the Nonya and Baba Restaurant in Singapore, where they put a little of the banana and cream into banana leaf envelopes and then chill the packages before serving. I've given an easier method here.

PREPARATION
Cut the banana into thin rounds and divide between 4 ramekins or small soufflé dishes.

In a pan, heat the coconut cream and stir in the rice flour, sugar and salt. Simmer until the mixture thickens.

Pour the mixture over the banana, then put into the refrigerator to cool and thicken before serving.

MAKING A MEAL

The recipes in this book can be divided into four categories:

A One-dish meals. These are usually noodle or rice dishes that are for quick eating -- lunch, snacks etc.

B Starters (hors d'oeuvre, appetizers, party-food). Traditional meals did not have separate courses, but it was usual for certain spicy dishes to be prepared first and brought out to be enjoyed with drinks before the rest of the meal was ready. Today, these are often used as hors d'oeuvre in the Western manner.

C Main courses. While there are some national variations, a well-planned meal anywhere in Southeast Asia consists of a group of dishes that create a harmonious balance of tastes and textures -- liquid and dry, hot and sweet, cooked and raw, soft and crisp, fried and steamed. There should also be a variety of ingredients: meat, fish, seafood and vegetables.

D Desserts. Most often a Southeast Asian meal ends with whatever fruits are in season. As in the West, however, the creation of many desserts is a specialist craft and they are more often bought than made at home. However, I have included a few easy recipes which can be used to enliven a dinner party.

VEGETARIAN MEALS

The symbol (♥) indicates that a dish is (or, with only slight alteration, could easily be made to be) suitable for vegetarians. I have included eggs and some recipes call for fish sauce, which can be replaced by light soy sauce. Almost all stir-fried meals can be converted by the simple procedure of dropping the meat listed in the ingredients and replacing it with an equal weight of coarsely chopped chunky-fleshed mushrooms. Many Southeast Asian vegetarians cook a meal for themselves, separating a little of the vegetarian version on a plate, then adding meat last for a second version for any non-vegetarian guests.

DRINKS

In most parts of Southeast Asia, cool water was traditionally drunk after a family meal. Except for Muslim Malaysia, men enjoying a night out would take bottles of spirits -- whisky or brandy -- to a restaurant to be drunk before, during and after the meal, much diluted with ice. For Vietnamese and Singapore nonya meals, Chinese tea would be an appropriate drink. Today, however, those that can afford them tend to drink Western drinks with their meals -- beer, Coca-Cola and, increasingly, wine.

While common-sense dictates that it would be foolish to serve a subtle vintage with a fiery curry, most robust characterful wines, especially those from Australasia, go well with most dishes in this book. With snacks and lunches from stalls and street-hawkers, it is common to see people drinking iced tea and iced coffee, though visitors are well advised to be wary of ice where there is any doubt as to the purity of the water from which it was made.

RECIPE LISTS AND MENU PLANS

The following is a guide to how the recipes can be broken down then recombined into a full meal for at least four people. If you have more guests, do not make extra amounts of these dishes but add some different ones from the lists. They are separated according to country to enable you to make an authentic Laotian or Burmese, etc., meal. There is much pleasure to be had, however, from picking out dishes from different countries and bringing them together as I have in the Southeast Asian feast that ends this section.

ONE-DISH MEALS

THAILAND

♥ **Pad Thai** (Thai Fried Noodles) page 47

♥ **Kow Tom Het** (Rice Soup with Mushrooms) page 41

LAOS

Nam Ngua (Lao Beef Noodle Soup with Mint Leaves) page 62

♥ **Tam Som** (Hot-and-sour Papaya Salad) page 67

CAMBODIA

♥ **Char Bai Mreah Priu** (Egg and Basil Fried Rice) page 88

Char Mee Gantang (Noodles with Pork and Eggs) page 91

♥ **Mee Char** (Vegetarian Egg Noodles) page 104

VIETNAM

Banh Khoai (Vietnamese Savoury Pancake) page 117

Pho Ga Hanh Xao (Chicken Noodle Soup with Crispy Shallots) page 119

Mi Xao Da Nang (Fried Noodles) page 119

Bun Thit Heo Nuong (Grilled Pork with Rice Vermicelli) page 120

BURMA

Wet-Tha Khauk-Swe-Gyaw (Stir-fried Noodles with Pork) page 153

Kyet-Tha Khauk-Swe-Byoke (Burmese Chicken Noodles) page 157

MALAYSIA AND SINGAPORE

Mee Hoon Goreng (Singapore Fried Noodles) page 180

Laksa Lemak (Spicy Noodle Soup) page 170

Kai Chok (Hainanese Chicken) page 173

STARTERS

(NB Salads and Soups from Main Courses may also be used as Starters)

THAILAND

Jin Ping (Grilled Marinated Pork) page 35

Tod Man Gung (Deep-fried Prawn and Sweetcorn Cakes) page 44

♥ **Tao Hu Tod** (Fried Fresh Beancurd with Sweet Nut Sauce) page 35

Gratong Mee Krob (Crispy Noodle Baskets) page 36

LAOS

Sai Ua Moo (Pork Sausage) page 68

CAMBODIA

Samlor Chanang Dy (Clay-pot Beef, Vegetables and Noodle Soup) page 93

VIETNAM

Nem Cuon Song (Fresh 'Nem' Spring Roll) page 122

▼ **Cha Gio Chay** (Vegetarian Spring Roll) page 125

Sa Suon Chien (Deep-fried Spare Ribs with Chilli and Lemon Grass) page 129

Cang Cua Chien (Deep-fried Crab-claws with Pork and Prawn Envelope) page 125

BURMA

▼ **Bayagyaw** (Spicy Split-pea Fritters) page 153

▼ **Pyaung-Bu Gyaw** (Fried Sweetcorn with Crispy Shallots) page 145

MALAYSIA AND SINGAPORE

Satay Ayam (Chicken Satay) page 179

MAIN COURSES

To create a substantial meal for four, select at least one dish from each category and serve with rice.

THAILAND

Dips and Sauces

Nam Prik Gung Pow (Grilled Shrimp Spice Dip) page 48

Soups

Tom Yam Gai (Chicken and Lemon Grass Soup) page 32

Salads

Yam Krabi (Krabi Seafood Salad) page 38

Mian Pla (Fish Ginger and Lime Salad) page 38

Curries

Gaeng Kiow Wan Nua (Beef in Green Curry with Coconut) page 40

Gaeng Luang Pla (Yellow Curry Fish) page 43

Penang Gai (Penang Dry Curry Chicken) page 40

Fried Dishes

Pad Prik King Nua Pad Bung (Fried Beef with Morning Glory) page 43

Pad Pet Moo (Stir-fried Pork with Curry Paste) page 41

Steamed Dishes

Gam Poo Op (Steamed Crab Claws) page 32

Pla Nung Manao (Steamed Fish with Lime) page 44

LAOS

For a more authentic Laotian meal it would be preferable – but not essential – to serve sticky rice.

Soups

▼ **Keng Bouad Mak Fak Kham** (Pumpkin in Coconut Soup) page 64

Ped Tom Kah (Duck and Galangal Soup) page 64

Keng Kalampi (White Cabbage Soup) page 62

Salads

Yam Kai Tom (Boiled Chicken Salad) page 74

Laap Ngua (Spicy Beef Salad) page 67

▼ **Soop Houa Phak** (Cooked Vegetable Salad) page 68

Curries

Kalee Ped (Duck Curry) page 73

Fried Dishes

Kai Jeun Na Som (Sweet-and-sour Fried Eggs) page 73

Sousi Pla (Spicy Coconut Fish) page 75

Kai Pad Mak Phet Deng (Fried Chicken with Red Chilli) page 77

Ngua Pad Mak Khe Ua (Fried Beef with Aubergine) page 75

Pad Som Sin Moo (Lemon Pork) page 77

▼ **Hed Pad Som Phak** (Mushrooms Fried with Pickled Cabbage) page 77

Steamed Dishes

Mok Pla (Fish Curry Steamed in Banana Leaf) page 70

CAMBODIA

Dips and Sauces

▼ **Tik Marij** (Cambodian Pepper Dip) page 91

Tik Prahok (Pickled Fish Dip) page 94

Soups

▼ **Samlor Jruoh** (Hot-and-sour Mushroom and Tomato Soup) page 93

Salads

Plea Saj Go (Hot-and-sour Beef Salad) page 99

Yoam Makah Trey Ang (Deep-fried Smoked Fish with Raw Mango Salad) page 94

Curries

Samlor Tik Tumpeang (Fish, Coconut and Young Bamboo Shoot Soup) page 100

Fried Dishes

▼ **Trop Bamporng Jiamuay Pong Tia** (Fried Aubergine with Egg) page 96

Saj Go Tik Prahok (Beef and Raw Vegetables with Pickled Fish Dip) page 99

Op Jumnee Jruk Bamporng (Sweet-and-sour Spare Ribs) page 96

Loclac (Stir-fried Pork with Salad and Tik Marij) page 101

Trey Pramar Jamhoy (Omelette with Pork and Pickled Fish) page 100

Muan Dot (Pot-roasted Chicken with Lemon Grass) page 88

Muan Char Khyey (Chicken with Ginger) page 103

Muan Char Kreung (Chicken Fried with Curry Paste) page 103

Steamed Dishes

Aamoh (Steamed Fish Curry) page 101

VIETNAM

Salads

Nom Du Du Thit Bo Nuong (Grilled Beef with Raw Papaya Salad) page 126

Goi Ga (Chicken Salad with Mint and Nuts) page 122

Fried Dishes

Cha Ca Nam (Grilled Fish with Mushroom Sauce) page 130

Bo Xao Mang (Beef with Bamboo Shoots) page 117

Than Chan Chanh (Kidneys with Mint and Lime) page 120

▼ **Dau Phu Xao Rau** (Beancurd with Stir-fried Mixed Vegetables) page 128

Chim Cuoc Chien (Deep-fried Quail) page 126

Bo Cau Roti (Grilled Pigeon) page 128

Steamed Dishes

Tom Hap Mien Dong (Prawn and Vermicelli Hotpot) page 128

Ca Hap Nam (Steamed Fish with Mushrooms) page 126

BURMA

Dips and Sauces

Ngan-Bya-Ye Dhyaw (Burmese Hot Sauce) page 146

Soups

Thakhwa-Thi Hin-Gyo (Cucumber and Dried Shrimp Soup) page 150

Salads

▼ **Khayan-Gyin-Thi-Thoke** (Tomato Salad) page 149

▼ **Mon-La-Doke-Thoke** (White Cabbage Salad) page 146

Nga-Pe Thoke (Hot-and-sour Fishcake Salad) page 146

Curries and Spiced Vegetable Dishes

Pazun Hin (Prawn Curry) page 149

▼ **Hmyit-Kyaw** (Bamboo Shoots Stir-Fried with Spice Paste) page 149

▼ **Khayan-Thi Pyot-Kyaw** (Fried Aubergine with Chilli and Shallots) page 149

Fried Dishes

Wet Tauk-Tauk Gyaw (Pork Fried with Dried Chilli) page 145

Ngar-Asat-Kyaw (Fried Fish with Crispy Chilli, Garlic and Shallots) page 150

Seik-Tha Hin (Lamb with Mint Leaves) page 154

Ametha Hin (Beef in Tamarind Sauce) page 157

▼ **Pe-Gyan-Gyaw** (Twice-cooked Split-peas) page 154

Be-Gin (Crispy Duck) page 154

MALAYSIA AND SINGAPORE

Dips, Sauces and Sambals

Sambal Kaehang Panjang (Prawn and Longbean Sambal) page 176

Sambal Ikan (Fish Sambal) page 176

Egg Sambal (Eggs in Spicy Tomato Sauce) page 179

Soups

▼ **Sup Tauhu** (Beancurd Soup) page 180

Salads

▼ **Gado Gado** (Vegetable Salad with Peanut Sauce) page 185

Curries

Rendang (Beef Rendang Curry) page 182

Fried Dishes

▼ **Roti** (Puffed Bread) page 182

Opor Ayam (Chicken in Coconut) page 185

Char Siew (Barbecued Pork) page 183

▼ **Nonya Chap Chai** (Nonya Mixed Vegetables) page 183

Daging Lembu Goreng Cina (Beef Stir-fried with Ginger and Spring Onions) page 173
Cili Ketma (Chilli Crab) page 175
Foo Yong Hai (Crab Meat and Bamboo Shoot Omelette) page 176

Steamed Dishes

Kerang Tumis Dengan Cili (Mussels with Onion, Garlic and Chilli) page 175

D E S S E R T S

T H A I L A N D

Kai Wan (Sweet Ginger Eggs) page 48
Kow Niew Tat (Sweet Sticky Rice Cakes) page 47

L A O S

Khao Tom Mak Kuay (Steamed Sticky Rice with Banana) page 78
Nam Van Loi Mak Teng (Melon in Coconut Milk) page 78

C A M B O D I A

Bai Damnerb Gruop Khano (Grilled Sticky Rice with Coconut and Jackfruit) page 104

V I E T N A M

Banh Chuoi (Banana and Sweet Potato Fritters) page 130
Che Dau Xanh (Moong Beans in Dark Sugar) page 129

B U R M A

Mon-Let-Saung (Sago with Palm Sugar and Coconut Milk) page 158
Kyauk-kyaw (Jelly Custard) page 158

M A L A Y S I A   A N D   S I N G A P O R E

Pulot Hitam (Black Sticky Rice Pudding) page 186
Kueh Pisang (Banana Pudding) page 186

S A M P L E   M E N U S

T H A I L A N D

Starters

Jin Ping (Grilled Marinated Pork) page 35
Tod Man Gung (Deep-fried Prawn and Sweetcorn Cakes) page 44

Main Courses

Yam Krabi (Krabi Seafood Salad) page 38
Gaeng Kiow Wan Nua (Beef in Green Curry with Coconut) page 40
Pla Nung Manao (Steamed Fish with Lime) page 44

Dessert

Kow Niew Tat (Sweet Sticky Rice Cakes) page 47

L A O S

Starters

Sai Ua Moo (Pork Sausage) page 68
Laap Ngua (Spicy Beef Salad) page 67

Main Courses

Ped Tom Kah (Duck and Galangal Soup) page 64
Ngua Pad Mak Khe Ua (Fried Beef with Aubergine) page 75
Hed Pad Som Phak (Mushrooms Fried with Pickled Cabbage) page 77
Mok Paa (Fish Curry Steamed in Banana Leaf) page 70
Sticky Rice page 11

Dessert

Nam Van Loi Mak Teng (Melon in Coconut Milk) page 78

C A M B O D I A

Starters

Samlor Chanang Dy (Clay-pot Beef, Vegetables and Noodle Soup) page 93
Yoam Makah Trey Ang (Deep-fried Smoked Fish with Raw Mango Salad) page 94

Main Courses

Samlor Tik Tumpeang (Fish, Coconut and Young Bamboo Shoot Soup) page 100
Trop Bamporng Jiamuay Pong Tia (Fried Aubergine with Egg) page 96
Jumnee Jruk Bamporng (Sweet-and-sour Spare Ribs) page 96
Muan Dot (Pot-roasted Chicken with Lemon Grass) page 88
Tik Marij (Cambodian Pepper Dip) page 91
Tik Prahok (Pickled Fish Dip) page 94

Dessert

Bai Damnerb Gruop Khano (Grilled Sticky Rice with Coconut and Jackfruit) page 104

V I E T N A M

Starters

Nem Cuon Song (Fresh 'Nem' Spring Roll) page 122
Cang Cua Chien (Deep-fried Crab-Claws with Pork and Prawn Envelope) page 125

Main Courses

Cha Ca Nam (Grilled Fish with Mushroom Sauce) page 130
Than Chan Chanh (Kidneys with Mint and Lime) page 120
Chim Cuoc Chien (Deep-fried Quail) page 126
Tom Hap Mien Dong (Prawn and Vermicelli Hotpot) page 128

Dessert

Che Dau Xanh (Moong Beans in Dark Sugar) page 129

B U R M A

Starters

Bayagyaw (Spicy Split-pea Fritters) page 153
Nga-Pe Thoke (Hot-and-sour Fishcake Salad) page 146

Main Courses

Pazun Hin (Prawn Curry) page 149
Wet Tauk-Tauk Gyaw (Pork Fried with Dried Chilli) page 145
Seik-Tha Hin (Lamb with Mint Leaves) page 154

Be-Gin (Crispy Duck) page 154
Ngan-Bya-Ye Dhyaw (Burmese Hot Sauce) page 146

Dessert

Kyauk-kyaw (Jelly Custard) page 158

M A L A Y S I A   A N D   S I N G A P O R E

Starters

Satay Ayam (Chicken Satay) page 179
Gado Gado (Vegetable Salad with Peanut Sauce) page 185

Main Courses

Sup Tauhu (Beancurd Soup) page 180
Rendang (Beef Rendang Curry) page 182
Opor Ayam (Chicken in Coconut) page 185
Cili Ketma (Chilli Crab) page 175

Rice

Roti (Puffed Bread) page 182

Dessert

Pulot Hitam (Black Sticky Rice Pudding) page 186

S O U T H E A S T   A S I A N   F E A S T

Canapés

Thailand – **Gratong Mee Krob** (Crispy Noodle Baskets) page 36
Burma – **Bayagyaw** (Spicy Split-pea Fritters) page 153
Malaysia & Singapore – **Satay Ayam** (Chicken Satay) page 179

Hors d'oeuvres

Vietnam – **Nem Cuon Song** (Fresh 'Nem' Spring Roll) page 122

Dips and Sauces

Cambodia – **Tik Marij** (Cambodian Pepper Dip) page 91
Burma – **Ngan-Bya-Ye** Dhyaw (Burmese Hot Sauce) page 146

Soup

Thailand – **Tom Yam Gai** (Chicken and Lemon Grass Soup) page 32

Salad

Laos – **Laap Ngua** (Spicy Beef Salad) page 67

Curry

Burma– **Khayan-Thi Pyot-Kyaw** (Fried Aubergine with Chilli and Shallots) page 149

Fried Dishes

Vietnam – **Chim Cuoc Chien** (Deep-fried Quail) page 126
Burma – **Seik-Tha Hin** (Lamb with Mint Leaves) page 154
Malaysia & Singapore – **Nonya Chap Chai** (Nonya Mixed Vegetables) page 183

Steamed Dish

Vietnam – **Ca Hap Nam** (Steamed Fish with Mushrooms) page 126

Desserts

Laos – **Nam Van Loi Mak Teng** (Melon in Coconut Milk) page 78
Malaysia & Singapore – **Kueh Pisang** (Banana Pudding) page 186

Bon Appetit!

INDEX